"So honest and real. A tear-je
Amy have a way of expressing the pain of loss yet are able
to honor their daughter with an incredible story that can
connect with just about anyone in some way or another."

-Allison, an engineer from Soddy Daisy, TN

"What a transparent, honest look at keeping faith and
hope during great tragedy. An inspirational reminder of
God's promises for the faithful and how to walk through
difficult times with grace and love."

**-Jamie, a school teacher and mother of four from
Ringgold, GA**

"This book reminds me that we all experience pain and
loss at some point in our lives. It has posed the question to
me now, 'How will I respond to that pain and loss?' I pray
I will respond with the same grace and strength that the
Carters have."

-Shannon, a pastor from Chattanooga, TN

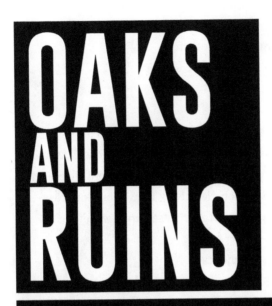

OAKS AND RUINS

LETTING GOD REDEEM YOUR LOSS

JASON
AND
AMY CARTER

Foresight Book Publishing
2435 Broad Street
Chattanooga, TN 37408
Visit ForesightPublishingNow.com

This book is dedicated to our beautiful Katie Beth. You lived life to the fullest and your love for others was unmatched. But it was your love for Jesus that touched so many people and that continues to impact the hearts and lives of so many. May your legacy of love continue on through these pages.

CONTENTS

ACKNOWLEDGEMENTS

We would like to thank our friends and family who have walked this incredibly painful journey with us. Your love and support have been instrumental in helping us survive many dark days. You have shown us the love of God in so many ways, and we are forever grateful.

Many thanks to Elaine and the team at Foresight Book Publishing Company for helping us share our story. We would not have been able to accomplish this without your guidance, wisdom, and encouragement along the way. Thank you for your patience, kindness, and sensitivity as we shared some of our most painful moments on this journey.

A special thanks to Jacob & Rachel Carter of Light Supply Company (www.lightsupply.co) for photography and design for the the cover of the book. Your creative gifts continue to bless and amaze us. Thank you for using them to honor us and God.

Last, but certainly not least, we praise the One who holds it all in His hands. To God, our Father, we give thanks above all. Thank you for your grace, your mercy, your faithfulness, your loving-kindness, and your unconditional love. Thank you for meeting us in the moment of our deepest need, in the midst of our greatest sorrow. Thank you for taking what the enemy meant for harm, and using it for a greater glory. Thank you for making us into Oaks, and giving us the opportunity to help rebuild the ancient ruins. You are worthy to be praised.

Isaiah 61:3-4[1]

And provide for those who grieve in Zion—
he will give them a crown of beauty
*   for ashes,*
the oil of joy for mourning,
and a garment of praise
*   for the spirit of despair.*
That they will be called oaks of righteousness,
a planting of the Lord for the display of his splendor.
And they will rebuild the ancient ruins
*   and restore the places long devastated;*
And they will renew the ruined cities that have been
*   devastated for generations.*

Oaks and Ruins? Smashed bricks surrounding an acorn? You're probably asking yourself what in the world that is all about. Well, for us it has been a huge part of our journey over the past 22 months or so, as you'll read in the pages that follow. This journey has had its share of heartache and pain, as well as a fair share of beauty and redemption. These two verses from the book of Isaiah have encouraged us, consoled us, and given us hope for the future. The deep promises of God held in these scriptures are beautiful and life-giving and make us excited for what God has in store. So, if you'll let us, we would like to take a few minutes and share how this passage has become the foundation for this book.

The entire chapter of Isaiah 61 is speaking to those who are broken and hurting. Verses 3-4 specifically point to what God will "provide for those who grieve." Grief is a crazy thing and can cripple you and lie to you; however, the very next phrase is a promise that we have clung to for over a year and a half, "He will give them a crown of beauty for ashes." Through our process of such great loss, this has been our prayer and our hope: that God will take our pain, our ashes, and make something beautiful out of it. What we have learned and what we read in this passage is that an exchange is necessary— "beauty FOR ashes," "oil of joy FOR mourning," and "a garment of praise FOR the spirit of despair." We must be willing to give the Father our brokenness and pain and allow Him to do with it as He sees fit. There's no promise that it'll be easy, but it's definitely worth the reward.

You see, this passage of scripture promises us redemption, but it also promises us that we are going to endure hardship. But Isaiah assures us that the struggles are not in vain. The verse tells us why: "That they will be called oaks of righteousness, a planting of the Lord for the display of his splendor." I don't think the oak tree was just randomly chosen out of all the trees to describe those who partner with God in the midst of their struggle. An oak tree has a deep tap root that brings the tree life giving water, but the oak's horizontal root system can occupy a space four to seven times the width of the tree's crown, providing incredible stability during storms. Even more, when oak trees are in close proximity to other oaks, they share root systems that graft together, making them even stronger.

This entire process begins with an acorn, the oak tree's fruit. Experts say that only one in ten thousand acorns will manage to develop into an oak tree. If acorns don't receive the water and care necessary, they will never germinate and develop into a tree. But given the right care and conditions, a tiny, seemingly insignificant acorn will turn into one of the mightiest and most beautiful trees on the planet. In other words, if we will make the exchange with God and link arms with others who are broken and hurting, He will make us into people who are strong and mighty, deeply rooted, all for the purpose of His glory!

The coolest part of this whole process is found in verse 4. If we give God our pain, not only will He make beautiful things from it and make us into Mighty Oaks, but He will use us to bring restoration to others: "And they will rebuild the ancient ruins and restore the places long devastated." What an incredible promise. He will bring restoration and healing to others through our pain. It is a remarkable thing that God's plan for changing the world and healing the hearts of wounded people is us...individuals who are also wounded, broken, and hurting.

So, regardless of the loss or pain you're going through, our desire is that you read the following pages through the lens of the promises found in Isaiah 61:3-4. Will you be the one in ten thousand? We believe you can. Turn to the Father and give Him your sorrow. Let your roots grow deep and wide. Look for how God wants to use your story to bring Himself glory and impact the lives of others for the Kingdom. We are no experts in the area of loss. We don't have all the answers. Others have experienced loss on a greater scale than us, for sure. But we felt compelled to share what we've learned along the way. There's more to our story and more to your story than just pain; God is up to so much more. We are living proof.

CHAPTER I

LOSS

"You will lose someone you can't live without, and your heart will be badly broken, and the bad news is that you never completely get over the loss of your beloved. But this is also the good news. They live forever in your broken heart that doesn't seal back up. And you come through. It's like having a broken leg that never heals perfectly—that still hurts when the weather gets cold, but you learn to dance with the limp."

- Anne Lamott

The Lord is close to the brokenhearted
and saves those who are crushed in spirit.

Psalm 34:18 [1]

{AMY}

On April 27, 1998, I gave birth to a sweet, beautiful 7 pound 4 ounce baby girl. This was our second child, and our first-born, Jacob Daniel, was 3 years old. We were all thrilled to have a girl in the family! We had carefully chosen her name, since we wanted to have a strong Biblical name, Katherine Elizabeth, Katie Beth for short. She was perfect, and I was thrilled to have a little girl to dress up and primp. Although I had been teaching for a few years already, my husband Jason and I decided it would be wise for me to stay home with Katie Beth and Jacob rather than pay for childcare for two children. It was not easy living on a single salary with a family of four, Jason's teacher's salary at that, but we were willing to make the necessary sacrifices so I could be home with the kids. I was able to do this for four years, and I am so grateful that we made that decision, especially now. That time was a gift; I would give just about anything to have those moments again.

Our family continued to grow when we added another baby girl, Kimberly Anne, to the Carter crew in 2000. She was not in our plans, but she was a part of God's plan for us. Shortly after she was born, I returned to teaching and our family continued to thrive. The kids grew older and developed their own personality and unique set of gifts, something Jason and I were blessed to witness. Jacob was the athlete, but had an artistic side to him as well. Katie Beth was our dancer and rule follower. Kimi was our musician with a fun-loving, free spirit.

We aren't a perfect family, and we certainly have our flaws, but each of us relies heavily on each other. Jason and I raised our children in church. A firm faith was something that was important to us, and in their own time, it became a vital element in each of our children's lives. We prayed together as a family. We shared our hurts and joys with one another. We played and laughed together. We have always been closely knit. We had our times of tension, sibling rivalry, and tears, but our love for each other continues to run deep and we always come back to that. We always wanted our children to know that their home was a safe place. We did our best to communicate this by simply being authentic, inside and outside of our home. Because Jason and I are both teachers, we feel a need to set an example for our now grown children as well as our students. Knowing that so many kids we come in contact with don't have stable home lives or healthy family dynamics, we want to be a light in any way we can. So, we genuinely try to live well and love well. This philosophy, living well and loving well, is one that we constantly encouraged in our home. Though they're not infallible, our kids strive to live this out every day. Katie Beth spent her life living and loving so, so well.

Like so many girls do, Katie Beth struggled through middle school with a sense of belonging and self-confidence. Although she was a part of the school dance team, she never felt pretty enough or good enough. We saw this insecurity, and we continually tried to encourage and reassure her that she was enough, because of who she was in God. Sometimes, though, the voices of doubt spoke louder than our truths. She began to have physical pain due to the anxiety in her life during this season—she spent many days in tears. I believe she felt the need to hide her struggles from most people because she tried to live an upbeat and positive life. We were thankful for our closeness as a family at times like this, because we were able to see the areas of insecurity that she tried to hide. As she searched for a niche to belong, she decided to become more involved with church activities and friends. She finally made a best friend and we were so thankful that she found someone who loved her well. Then high school started.

We had hoped high school would be better for Katie Beth, and it was... a little. She continued to dance and hoped to make the varsity team her junior year. Even though she was deeply committed to the school dance team the previous five years, had taken private lessons, and attended studio classes, she was not selected for the varsity team. This rejection was a blow that I wasn't sure she, or I, would recover from. She was truly devastated and my heart hurt for her. Other girls from the team were shocked she didn't make it. It didn't make sense to us, but sometimes, God's plans are different than our plans.

We decided to go a different direction and found a professional studio in a nearby city. We enrolled her in classes there, and she was chosen to be a part of their competitive dance team. The next two years of training and relationships she gained were priceless. She regained her love for dance and her self-confidence was restored. She made dear friends and we know

now that God closed the school dance door so she would be able to walk through the Scenic City Dance door instead. We believe the training she received there prepared her to achieve her dream of dancing in college.

Though the school dance team door was closed, another opportunity at school opened for Katie Beth when she was asked to be a manager for the football team. Even though she had grown up watching Jacob play football, we weren't sure if she would enjoy this job. We couldn't have been more wrong! She loved it. She felt needed and she loved that. She handled important matters for coaches, but also took care of the players. She was kind of like a team mom. During games, she always fixed the boys' pads if they were sticking out of their jerseys or sleeves for some reason. While she enjoyed her position as a manager, it was difficult for her to see the dance team on the sidelines every Friday night. Eventually, though, she realized God had given her a greater assignment. We realize now that God was expanding her territory before she left us.

Fast forward. KB, as we affectionately called her, made the decision, after several college visits, to attend Jacksonville State University in Alabama. We could tell almost immediately that she loved the campus, and everything about the school, when we went on a tour. She found JSU's renowned dance line, The Marching Ballerinas, to be appealing too. We discussed the possibility of her not making the team, due to her previous experience, but she said she wanted to attend JSU even if she didn't make it. I'll never forget the moment she walked up to that famous "boot" and saw her name; she was a JSU Marching Ballerina! All the pain of previous rejections disappeared, and she was fully alive. She had achieved her dream.

There is something magical about seeing your child bloom like a beautiful flower, especially after struggling through storms. Making new friends, living her dream of dancing in college, confidently facing her future... it was so beautiful to watch, especially after all the previous struggles. In just a few short summer months, during Ballerina rehearsals, she formed some very close relationships. People accepted and loved her just the way she was. She was learning dances alongside other girls who loved to dance as much as she did. Because she graduated high school with 44 college credits, she was able to immediately begin classes in the education department, as she felt called to teach children. She was happier than we had ever seen her, and we could tell simply by her eyes and smile. When I went to see her dance at the first football game of the season, I was speechless. I thought, *Oh my goodness, she is absolutely radiant!*

KB came home the next day, after that first game, to visit for Labor Day weekend. She went to the high school she'd attended to visit coaches, teachers, and friends. She got to spend some quality time with her best friend Madison and other church friends. Kimi and Jacob were both performing that weekend at two different gigs, and KB was thrilled to be able to support them in person. That Sunday, we spent the morning at church and then headed to the grocery store to buy groceries and goodies for her to take back to school with her. And, per her request, the five of us had a family game night—KB's favorite source of family fun.

The next day, it was time for her to head back to JSU. She and her "band squad" friends had plans to watch the sunset together that night when they all returned back to campus. We gave hugs, said our goodbyes, took some pictures, and walked her out to her car. In typical Carter fashion, we all obnoxiously waved and danced in the driveway as she pulled out. Little did we know, that would be the last time we ever saw her.

Later that afternoon, I was home alone and I suddenly felt something was wrong. Call it mother's intuition, discernment, or whatever you wish, but there was an uneasiness in my soul. I realized that I probably should have heard from KB by that point. When any of us were traveling, it was our routine to let each other know when we arrived safely. I tried calling her. No answer. I quickly became very anxious, because I had that uneasy feeling. I tried calling her again. No answer. Then I tried to call her roommates. She wasn't there. Then I tried to call a Ballerina friend. Nothing. At this point, panic was setting in. Jacob arrived home and we decided we needed to go get Jason and Kimi from softball practice to help us figure out what was going on. We began calling police, family, and other friends. No news. Then our phone rang.

{JASON}

As we were standing in our dining room attempting to locate Katie Beth, I could feel panic setting in. That is the moment I had an incoming call from Katie Beth's cell number. Grady Hospital, in Atlanta, was on the line. They told us they had KB and the doctors were with her. She had been in a severe car accident with an 18-wheeler and had been life-flighted there. We immediately flew out the door to drive two grueling hours to Grady. We decided to meet my parents at a local fast food restaurant off the interstate to ride together. While we were waiting for them to arrive, the phone rang again. This time it was a doctor from Grady. He confirmed that I was Katie Beth's dad and then the following exchange took place:

"Mr. Carter are you driving?"

"No, but we are about to be on the road headed that way."

"Mr. Carter are you sitting down?

"No, no, no...Please, don't tell me that?"

"I'm sorry Mr. Carter, but she was dead on arrival."

I immediately fell to my knees, head in the grass, continually pleading, "Oh my God, please no!" Of course, at that point Amy, Jacob, and Kimi knew that we had lost Katie Beth and I can only imagine what the scene looked like to others in that parking lot. In those moments lying in the grass, I can vividly remember thinking that I literally would not survive this pain. It was as if I had been kicked in the stomach and all the life in me had gone with it. As I stood up to check on my family, I witnessed, in that same patch of grass, the people I love the most in this world reeling in agonizing pain. Jacob and Kimi sat in the grass overcome by grief and tears. Amy was just a few feet away from me sitting on the ground in hopeless tears. The feeling of helplessness was overwhelming because I knew that there was nothing I could say or do to comfort them or fix their brokenness.

My mom and dad arrived to find this scene and immediately knew exactly what was going on. Together, we made the decision to travel to Grady in Atlanta. Amy and I were in the middle seat of my parents' van and our kids were in the back. In those first minutes of that ride no one spoke, the only sounds were that of crying and the deafening sound of silence. It was the type of silence that only deep grief brings. But out of the silence and tears, something happened that will forever be etched in our hearts and minds. Through her tears and brokenness, Kimi began to sing the chorus of the song "Good Good Father":

> *You're a good good father*
> *It's who you are, it's who you are, it's who you are*
> *And I'm loved by you*
> *It's who I am, it's who I am, it's who I am*

To hear our 15 year old daughter proclaim that truth, in that moment, was incredible, yet difficult. He didn't seem all that good if I'm honest, but in the coming days, weeks, and months, the memory of that moment would carry me through some dark days and be one of the things that would help me believe the truth in those lyrics. At that time, I couldn't imagine the journey that was before me, because deep loss, and the grief that comes with it, has a tendency to blur and distort all that you once believed to be true and right. The days to come would prove to be extremely dark and challenging, to say the least. I will never forget Amy saying to me when we finally made it home from Grady Hospital that night, "I just don't want our pain to be wasted."

On September 5, 2016, our world changed forever. We lost one of the people we love the most in this world. It was, and is, the kind of loss I never expected. The kind of loss that should only happen in movies; I thought it only happened to other people. This time, though, the tragedy was ours. Thus began our journey with loss, deep sorrow, and unspeakable pain. Nothing could have prepared us for this and the journey that followed. Even now, nearly two years later, the pain is still very intense. Some days are worse than others. Some days, though, we see the beauty amidst the sorrow.

Though it's still fresh, there have been some things we've learned from experiencing such unthinkable loss. Therefore, we feel compelled to share these loss lessons. You will be able to relate, even if your circumstance is not the same as ours. Loss is loss—loss of dreams, a loved one, a marriage, a job—whatever it may be. It has a way of touching everyone in some shape or form. Some people try to compare or measure loss in relation to others, but we believe it hurts regardless of how it looks. Granted, losing our daughter is by far the most difficult thing we have ever experienced, and hopefully ever will. It's so hard to describe to those who haven't experienced it. And yet, I wouldn't wish this kind of loss on anyone—not even my greatest enemy. In some ways, I wish I could put the pain into words, but then again, there really are no words.

The following chapters are the lessons God has taught us along the way. We want to share these with you as a way to encourage you on your journey, whatever that path may be. Some of you may have walked a painful path similar to ours, while others may have experienced a different kind of loss. Either way, our hope is that these lessons from loss will minister to your heart and remind you that there can be *beauty for ashes*, that we are all justified in processing pain uniquely, and that you are not alone.

REFLECTION QUESTIONS:

- What type of loss have you experienced or are you currently walking through?
- In what ways has this loss affected you? (physically, spiritually, emotionally, etc.)
- How have you processed the pain your loss has inflicted? Has that brought hope to you or has it deepened the pain?

CHAPTER II

LISTEN

"Listening to God—which is a key part of practicing
His presence—
is not a method, but a walk with a person."
- Leanne Payne

The hearing ear and the seeing eye—
the Lord made them both.
Proverbs 20:12[1]

HEARING AND LISTENING {JASON}

Listening is a lost art. We live in a world where everyone has something to say or an opinion to share. How many times are we simply thinking about our response to what someone is saying to us instead of focusing on what they are trying to tell us? Understanding how to *truly* listen comes through first understanding the difference between hearing and listening. Hearing is something that occurs because we have ears and someone is talking to us. When we hear, words and noises make their way to our ears and our minds simply to alert us that a sound exists. Listening is a whole different ball game. You have to choose to listen, to really focus in on what the other person is trying to communicate. When we *truly* listen to someone, we get the message beyond the words. These are the conversations that aren't simply filed away in our head, but those that find refuge in our hearts.

If you're the one walking through pain or loss, listening means hearing the hearts of those who attempt to speak words that are meant to comfort you. Their words at times may be shallow or even foolish, but listening means choosing to hear their heart—a heart that, in most cases, is sincere and good. For the person who is navigating the road of trying to help a friend or family member during their time of grief, the best advice we can give is to listen before speaking. Don't feel as if you have to come up with the "right words." Words won't fix the situation or the pain, but a compassionate heart that is content in simply being present and listening brings comfort. Not to mention, truly listening helps you discern the best way to respond.

{AMY}

We will always remember and appreciate those who reached out sincerely and out of love after Katie Beth passed away. The emotions we experienced were on a caliber we didn't even know existed. No condolence, though, no matter how sincere, could permanently console us. And, at times, I would rather hear the honest "I don't know what to say," than the pressured spout of empty words conjured up by obligated friends. In desperately trying to empathize with a situation they were disconnected from or a situation God had not directed them to, their attempts fell short of effective. Even when I smiled and said "Thank you", empty words did more harm than good.

So what does this mean? Do you have a place in consoling a friend who lost a job when you've worked for the same company for 20 years? Yes. Are you exempt from caring for a family who just lost a father? No. Should you avoid hugging that friend at the funeral because you don't know what it's like to lose a family member? Absolutely not.

Understanding the difference between empathy and sympathy can be a frustrating endeavor. It can make you feel disconnected and unrelatable to the person you're wishing to comfort. For whatever reason, you may be unable to empathize, but know that your sympathy is enough. Your presence is enough. And, yes, it's needed.

SYMPATHY VERSUS EMPATHY {JASON}

Showing sympathy, generally speaking, is an action I'd describe as *feeling for*, while empathy is *feeling with*. I've heard Amy say that sympathy cards are what line the card aisle at the store, not empathy cards. It's an awkward thing to explain, because one expression isn't less important than the other, and both elements are needed when processing and helping someone through trials. For instance, someone may feel sorrow *for* us because we lost Katie Beth; someone else may feel sorrow *with* us because they, too, have lost a daughter. I find it hard to relate to someone's loss or pain if I haven't experienced that same loss, but I can't say that empathy is exclusive only to those who have parallel experiences. To me, the most empathetic situations have come from those who truly understood the road we were walking—and are walking—or at least put themselves in our shoes and attempted to feel our pain.

Recently, a close friend reached out to me concerning a friend of his who had lost a 22 year old daughter unexpectedly. This friend of mine asked if he could give his friend my contact information in order to possibly help him walk through the loss. I was happy to do this, but what stood out to me was my friend's reasoning and wisdom. You see, this friend of mine lost his father years before to suicide and told me that he recently had the opportunity to help a couple of people who were experiencing the same thing. And though his loss was devastating and difficult, he understood that his capacity to empathize with his friend was limited because he had never lost a child. He was wise and recognized that he could offer sympathy, but what his friend also needed was someone who would know exactly the thoughts, feelings, struggles, and pain he was and would be experiencing.

For those who feel like they have little to give because their well of compassion is running dry, or for those who feel that they cannot do enough, take comfort in what John Eldredge says: "The human soul was not built for carrying the heartache of the world. Only Jesus can do that."[2]

FINDING CONNECTIONS {AMY}

Amidst the mixture of both well-intentioned and poorly executed sympathies, the exhaustion of constantly nodding my head and exhaling stale *thank yous* digressed when I shared my pain with those who understood our loss. I call these soul-ties, because that's what they feel like: an allowance to connect, share, and grieve on the same deep level.

We both continually ask: *Why?* And as parents, we'd silently added to it, in our own minds, secretly understanding the other's pain: *Was our loss worth this lesson?* To know that other parents have asked, and continue to ask, the same questions is a freeing experience.

Instead of a funeral, we chose to have a celebration of life for Katie Beth. Many people showed up to Katie's service. Some of them I met for the first time; I had no idea who they were or how they knew our daughter. We were blessed to have people from all over come to celebrate Katie and comfort us that day—so many that we weren't even able to greet everyone.

Local friends, students who knew Katie Beth through school or dance, our friends from college whom we hadn't seen in years, and people we didn't even know crowded together that day to offer their support. A couple we had never met made their way through the line, shook our hands, and told us that they had lost their daughter. To this day, I couldn't tell your their names or point them out in a crowd, but I'll forever remember their words. "We don't know you and we don't know your daughter," the wife said, "but we've lost our daughter. We know the pain you're feeling and we just wanted to come and pay our respects, encourage you, and to let you know that you're not alone." In a room full of people we knew, some our entire lives, the words of these fellow suffering parents offered a subtle relief.

We never imagined we'd be the suffering parents who understood another parent's loss. "All I can say is 'I'm sorry,'" Jason told me one day. It's so simple, but this resonated with me because it's so true. Even though it took us each a few months after her accident to even realize that we *could* relate with others, we knew what it meant to us to have those who'd gone before us share their experiences. The only initial words that we had to offer that wouldn't radiate false positivity and discomfort were simply "I'm sorry." Though previously unimaginable, we knew this was a new, yet hard, way to serve others.

A cancer patient would rather be mentored by a cancer survivor than a perfectly healthy athlete. A cancer survivor can provide the good, bad, and the ugly. Anyone can offer hope, but a survivor knows what a current patient needs to hear, because they have a better idea of what cancer is, how it feels, and how it transforms a life. When you train on a job, you are trained by someone who understands how the company generally works. When I teach, I'm facilitating a learning process for my students—a process I already understand.

While our condolences, as parents who have lost a child, are not more important than those who haven't experienced this type of loss, they are unique. After losing Katie, we reconsidered the losses our friends had experienced. Because our perception was now entirely different after experiencing our own agonizing heartbreak, we better understood the losses we'd formerly been somewhat disconnected from.

In instances like this, instead of feeling like we were in a boat in the middle of the ocean, with no paddles and completely alone, we saw ripples from all different directions meeting those of our own. Patterns began to emerge, intertwine, and connect. These ripples provided a refuge of sorts, a community we could depend on—a promise that we weren't alone.

REMEMBER WHAT IS TRUE

In his interview with Pastor Greg Laurie, Steven Curtis Chapman[3] discusses experiencing this same disconnect when he lost his 5 year old daughter, Maria. He explained that people tried to say the right words, only to prove that they didn't know what to say. Though it's an interview, it sounds more like a conversation between Laurie and Chapman. At one point Laurie, who also lost a child of his own, relates, " I've heard, 'I know what you're going through, I lost my grandmother.' I don't want to insult

them, but I want to say 'Grandmothers die, children aren't supposed to.'"
At first his response sounds rough, but he's got a point.

Chapman sympathizes with those who struggle to connect. "We've all stood in that place," he says. "I'm usually the one walking down the aisle, toward the family who's lost someone and I'm thinking 'God, what do I say?'" He then explains that what has proven to be the most comforting through his family's loss are the words from friends who ironically express "There are no words." According to Chapman, that was comforting and encouraging because people were able to acknowledge that his family's loss was way deeper than any words they could provide.

Psalm 42:9-11[4]
9 I will say to God, my rock,
"Why have You forgotten me?
Why must I go about in sorrow
because of the enemy's oppression?"
10 My adversaries taunt me,
as if crushing my bones,
while all day long they say to me,
"Where is your God?"
11 Why am I so depressed?
Why this turmoil within me?
Put your hope in God, for I will still praise Him,
my Savior and my God.

During this interview, Chapman references Psalm 42 to discuss the desperation for a solid foundation in the Lord. At the beginning of this Psalm, David is heavily examining his position in a place where he feels far from God, away from pure worship, and possibly forgotten. "Come on heart, remember what is true," Chapman paraphrases. He explains that David is preaching to himself through this expression. The end of verse 11 is pivotal in this passage, as David reminds himself that his hope is in God, his praise is for God, and his salvation is from God.

Though David was experiencing a different type of loss, we understand his process of questioning God. He asks desperate, sincere questions. It seems, in verse 11, that he realizes that he isn't listening to what he knows to be true. It took a while, but we also consistently asked *why me?* before we said *Come on heart!* and remembered what was true: He is good and He is for us.

AVOID THE UNKNOWN: DIFFERENTIATING THE MYSTERIES FROM THE MEMORIES {JASON}

In most aspects of life, we are encouraged to embrace the unknown, or to not be fearful of it. However, in relation to loss, the unknown is a murky, toxic, unidentified substance. The unknown, in this case, is the hypothetical. Particular to death, all elements are hardly ever revealed to us. Amy and I believe this is because of the Lord's perfect timing. Christ reveals truths to us as we are able to handle them.

In our case, questioning what happened in those few minutes before Katie was killed in her accident does nothing beneficial for us. We can't know. Even if we did know, there's nothing we could do to change what happened. That, in and of itself, is hard enough. It took us a long time to reconcile the fact that God is potentially saving us from these details.

I came to realize that the mysteries and the memories are different. As humans we tend to want answers. Part of me wants to know what caused the wreck, what happened, and what it looked like. I ask myself why the driver didn't swerve and miss her car. Was the truck driver possibly impaired or distracted? Overworked? Tired? A million questions would invade my brain if I allowed them to. Sure, some questions need to be addressed, but this doesn't mean that they will be answered, or that they need to be.

That being said, I don't believe that there are pieces of reality that should be avoided. Just like a physical wound, healing doesn't come unless you acknowledge the wound, nurse it, and treat it. And, in the end, wounds often leave scars. A doctor can't avoid a wound and successfully bring wholeness. It may heal temporarily, but it won't heal correctly. If it's improperly treated, it will reopen and cause additional attention and pain.

FOR THE HURTING {AMY}

Know that you're not alone. I'm not saying this to diminish your pain. Because of our faith, Jason and I never believed we were alone, despite the lies that impeded our daily lives. But, for those who do not believe as we do, you still are not alone. There are so many possibilities for support, whether it's other grieving parents, recovery groups, counseling, and more; there are endless resources for people who have suffered loss. It has ministered to my heart to be a part of some of these groups.

At the time of your loss, maybe it's easiest to remain silent. You don't owe anyone anything. Although, there's no shame or lack of tact in reconnecting with those who touched you during your experience, even if you didn't let them know how much they mattered then. It's likely that those who made an impact know that you have nothing left to give or that you're hurting so deeply that you don't know how to respond to encouragement, prayer, or direction. But, reconnect with those people who have been consistently available, those who reached out to you and made an impact. Let them know you're grateful, that you're ready to talk or process, or that you're lost and unsure where to turn.

Don't Suffer in Solitude

Jason has warned friends of ours against digging a hole and jumping in it. For him, he says, this would be sitting in his recliner, entertained by anything that would kidnap his emotions. For me, though, this looks like a full planner, with every minute of the day scheduled with something to keep myself busy. Being alone has the potential to be dangerous. A lot of people choose to suffer alone and become enveloped by the darkness of grief.

Moments of solitude are definitely necessary, but they shouldn't be the only time you allow yourself to grieve. Whether it's healthy or unhealthy, selfish or not, I *need* these moments alone. Sometimes this involves joyful tears while flipping through photo albums or remembering a conversation I'd had with Katie after encountering something that reminds me of her. Other times, being alone looks like talking myself down and exhausting my anger with a long walk around my neighborhood. As good as these moments of solitude feel, they'll become harder and harder to manage. Thoughts will begin to control my actions and emotions. Societally and spiritually, we aren't designed to live life alone; so, why would we be asked to suffer alone? We weren't meant to.

One of my favorite writers and speakers, Havilah Cunnington, says a bit about the danger of suffering alone, in her blog.[5] "One of the greatest traps of doing HARD THINGS is the 'Why Me?' trap," she explains. "It's a place where the enemy wants us to believe that God somehow actually gave us more than we could handle. He wants us to believe that instead of God being a good Father to us, we are left to depend on ourselves. The enemy tries to convince us that God is not a present Papa but rather a forgetful Father... The enemy likes us to stay in our pit. He will try to get us to buy into any lie he can in order to keep us bound, never victorious, and always feeling defeated." Truthfully, it's a lie I have to constantly renounce. For the questions I don't have answered, I have to trust that God is steadily revealing those answers to me as I am able to handle them. And, in turn, this means that I may not ever have all the answers.

"The enemy knows that if he can get us to take these HARD THINGS as a personal assault from God, we will no longer believe that He is a good God but a lying and deceitful God, who likes to punish His people," she continues. "If we believe this lie, we will stay in the pit and our inner lives become dark and cold without hope. We have to identify the 'why me?' lie and understand it is a trap that will try to keep us bound. Once we recognize it as a trap, it empowers us to no longer nurture our fallen souls with 'why me?' but empower our spirits with 'why not' and to climb out of the pit and move forward."

In a paragraph or two, Havilah makes handling pain sound easy. Having listened to several of her talks, I know that she is not belittling my pain or suggesting that I "move forward" quickly or simply. Having lived this exact scene that she describes though, I know that by the time the exhaustion has set in from digging and jumping into the pit, getting ourselves out requires help.

As Jason and I are both teachers, analogies and metaphors are strategies we use every day to make a concept easier to understand. Some long time friends of ours gave us a book titled *Tear Soup*.[6] In the book, which appears to be a child's book with its colorful illustrations and large print, authors Pat Schwiebert and Chuck DeKlyen carefully and generally approach the topic of loss. With the analogy of making soup, they show that soup can take a long time to stew, just as grief can take a long time to process. They note that different people may impose and try to make the soup for the cook, instead of assisting the cook in the tasks she needs to complete. The ingredients that fill the pages relate to the many elements that are present when processing loss: good and bad memories, sadness and happiness, isolation and comfort, and more.

Jason and I have moments of solo soup making. Like we mentioned earlier, at times, we believed the lie that we were alone even when together. Then there are moments when it's a couple's effort, as well as those moments when friends and family add their tears to the recipe. Even when we were certain that our friends couldn't understand what we felt, we were aware of those who were consistently there for us. For the person in solitary grief, who perhaps doesn't accept any of your offerings, keep loving them and be consistently available. Small gestures mean so much. If you're this person, know that it is okay to take your time. Eventually though, you will feel more and more isolated if you do not accept the support that's available to you. Jason, myself, and our two kids were blessed to have support bombarding us from every angle. This may not be the case for everyone; however, like I said earlier, there are numerous resources available for all types of loss. Seek them out, try them out—yes, more than once—and be poured into.

Every day for over a year following Katie's accident, I had one friend who sent me three simple emojis. Her message always arrived at a different time of day. Most of the time I didn't respond, but it was okay, because she didn't expect conversation. You see, this friend knows great loss quite well herself. Her daily messages were a reminder that she was thinking of us and continuing to love and support us. She was, and is, a great example of someone who was "listening" well. Most of Jason's friends who were consistent through the process were respectful of our space. Our friend Wally said once, "I don't know what to say. I can't imagine." Like the couple who shared their loss with us at Katie's celebration of life, this meant much more to us than simply the words that were spoken. This kind of honest support, paired with those who did understand, indirectly said "I love you and I hurt for you, but I've got nothing for you." These words showed us that a person was praying for us and committing to walking some portion of the road with us.

Then, sometimes support comes in other ways, ways that are completely unexpected. After we lost Katie Beth, we were flooded with cards, gifts, conversations, and messages from people who told us what Katie meant to them. Of course we thought our daughter was wonderful, but it was truly touching to hear that she actually was the joy we saw her to be to so many people.

After her accident, we received a letter from a young lady who interacted with KB at a dance competition. Apparently, she had only spent time with Katie at that event. At some point during the competition weekend, Katie connected with this young woman; she told us in the letter that, during the competition, she was going through a dark time that had led her to contemplate suicide. We don't know if Katie knew about this young woman's struggle, or if she had just befriended her over the weekend. But, we do know, thanks to this woman's vulnerability, that Katie had intentionally sought her out. "Your daughter touched my life," she wrote.

Some might say that Katie's humility is what prevented us from knowing details like this in her life, but the truth is that living intentionally and loving well was Katie's norm. In other words, this was nothing out of the ordinary for her. We're lucky enough to have notes and shared memories like these. Not everyone is and we recognize that. I imagine things would have been radically different for us if we hadn't received this kind of support. Some people lose their child before they even leave the womb, so they may not receive this same kind of comfort, but that certainly doesn't mean their life didn't matter. Every life matters.

Those moments are so valuable to us, but even in the case that we didn't receive these written moments from strangers, we can rest in knowing that Katie Beth affected more lives than ours. Grab those moments and hold to them dearly. Store them away in your mind and file through them frequently. Remember the good. We choose to dwell on the memory of Katie Beth's life, not her death.

There are people who surround you in the moment of loss, and they are needed, but there are also people who are going to walk the long road with you. Each of those people, those who are present immediately and those who stay, serve a unique, necessary, and beautiful purpose. So many people prayed with us, cooked food, provided gift cards for meals out, and more. And now, we look up and we see the people who are still here. This doesn't discredit the people who helped first hand, but some friends are in for the long haul.

Initially, you'll undoubtedly need the huge flock to help you function. As the trauma and pain distances, though, you only need a few of the flock. You need people there to support you and hold you up when you have tough days.

Be Cautious

This is something that possibly isn't addressed enough. Some people reached out to us through social media to share their condolences, while others reached out to let us know they had been at the scene of the accident and done their best to help. We were grateful to hear from some of these, but our hearts were quite vulnerable, as you can imagine. In my moments of vulnerability, I allowed someone to enter into those sacred places of my heart that were longing and searching for answers. Instead of accepting the unknowns of Katie Beth's accident, I fell into the trap of believing lies that were told to me by a stranger at the scene. Another stranger sent a graphic message through social media to our daughter Kimi about seeing Katie's car at the accident site. I'm not sure why these people felt it necessary to say and do these things, but it certainly didn't make our journey any easier.

Because of this, I want to address anyone experiencing loss: guard your heart. For the most part, people's motives are pure; they want to minister to someone in pain and in need. Then there are others who want to insert themselves into the loss and pain. Instead of feeling empathy, they feel some type of identity vicariously through someone else's pain. It makes no sense to me as to why people would want to do this, but this unnecessary pain can cause a lot of damage. They may not realize it, but people who choose to "help" in this way are, in a sense, only exponentially multiplying the heartache, grief, and sorrow.

"EVERYTHING HAPPENS FOR A REASON" {JASON}

Our deepest condolences go out to you and your family.

Take comfort knowing she's in a better place.

We're so sorry.

When my cat passed, I just didn't know what to do.

I'm sorry for your loss.

She's with the Lord.

You'll see her again one day.

I lost my grandmother last year, I know this is hard.

So many people offer condolences, some more sincere than others. If you've been in the receiving line, you know that it's not always easy to accept all the sympathies that are offered your way. Even though I knew "Everything happens for a reason" and we believed "Katie is in a better place," the disgruntled, sarcastic, and haphazard "Yeah, thanks!" or "Good grief, we know!" that I wanted to belt out in response just didn't seem to be suitable.

If you find that you're the one doing the consoling, here's a nugget of wisdom: don't state the obvious. No matter how "insightful" it may seem to you at the time, the individual who experienced the loss knows the obvious. In fact, they're probably painfully aware. Learn to listen and hear that pain instead of trying so hard to offer "words of wisdom" that are emptier than you think. Later, work through the obvious with them, readily admitting your difficulty to understand it as well.

At times, it felt like people attempted to relate out of obligation. We truly heard everything from relating our daughter's death to the loss of a cat to the loss of a job. Like we've said before, everyone experiences, or will experience, loss to some extent; but, in recalling the responses we received, some people's words are remembered more than others, and sometimes not in a positive light.

Point blank, we can't fix or eliminate each other's pain. And in the same way, though we may experience loss like another parent, there's nothing we can say to fill their obvious void. So, whether you're receiving sympathetic or empathetic expressions, know that people are well intentioned. Maybe a "Thank you" is all you can offer. Maybe you can't respond. Know that whatever you're feeling is okay. Sometimes you have to choose to hear the heart of the person rather than their clumsy, "comforting" clichés. It's all a part of the learning process of walking through this journey.

REFLECTION QUESTIONS:

- Have you experienced firsthand the struggle between sympathy and empathy? What are some unforced ways that you can minister to someone in their time of loss?
- Have you walked through a "Why me?" time in your life? How did God help you walk through those hard things? How did those times deepen your faith and reliance on God?
- Have you ever had the opportunity to reach out to someone who is hurting or grieving because of your previous experience with a similar pain? How did that help you and/or them in helping to heal that pain?

CHAPTER III

LOOK

"One sees great things from the valley, only small things from the peak."

- G. K. Chesterton

I pray that the eyes of your heart may be enlightened in order that you may know the hope to which he has called you, the riches of his glorious inheritance in his holy people...

Ephesians 1:18[1]

CONTROLLING YOUR GAZE {BOTH}

To put it simply, reflecting on life post-loss is like driving. You have your rearview mirror and you use it to look back, making sure that things are clear and there's nothing behind you that's going to be a hindrance to you. Even though you're moving forward and looking through the windshield, there are times when you *have* to look in the rearview mirrors so that you will be aware of the things that are going on around you, in order to be safe and effective in getting to where you're supposed to go. At the same time, though, glancing in the rearview mirror is a reminder that you're not headed that way.

Considering that metaphor, if we chose to stare in the rearview, we'd be focusing too much on what *has happened* and not what it *is becoming*. Focusing too much on the loss or the effects of the loss, or as our counselor Mark calls it "sitting in the puddle," is dangerous to our hearts, our emotions, and our relationships. As a couple, if one of us chose to live in that pain every day, our marriage would shatter. Marriage is already challenging enough without trauma; when one person refuses to process, it's a tough place to be. For us, this meant committing to months of counseling, relying daily on Christ, and communicating our pain with each other as best we could.

In relating to loss, picture a photo album. Its purpose is to look back, reflecting on memories. It often sits stored away in a closet, out on a coffee table, or being prepared in a craft room. Looking at a photo album inspires you to relive and value memories. But, if all you ever did was look through a photo album and reminisce, you'd miss out on the opportunity to take more pictures and make more memories to value. Sure, I (Jason) sit and look at old photos of Katie Beth where she's doubled over in the floor laughing at something someone said. In that moment, I hear her deep, completely unbefitting laugh; I remember us jokingly mocking it as it bellowed out of her small body. I see pictures of her dance team days, where she smiled through strained positions and choreography. In a sense, it's comforting to remember the positive things that exist alongside our pain. There are so many times I find myself looking through literally hundreds of pictures of Katie Beth I have saved in my phone or home videos that we have of her when she was younger. There is always a moment if I stay there too long where I can feel myself moving from healthy reminiscing to planting myself in a pretty deep hole that I won't want to climb out of. It is in those times I have to keep my eyes open to what is happening in my own heart and mind because if I don't, my gaze will be solely on my pain and I will become despondent, cold, and closed off, especially to those that need me the most.

Think again about the mirrors, in relation to their sizes compared to the windshield. The sheer difference in the size suggests another analogy. You're endangered if you ignore the safety mirrors, but further endangered if they're all you pay attention to. In relation to loss, we must be aware of how reflection will affect our journey. These driving tools are used primarily for glancing. We use the mirrors systematically, glancing back for a specific purpose. Similarly, our memories are tools for active and healthy reflection. Don't abuse them.

ENGAGING THE FIVE SENSES {JASON}

Amy calls mashed potatoes her "comfort food." It was the first and only thing we could get her to eat in the initial days following Katie's accident. Friends and family were begging her to eat something, and she finally agreed to a few bites of mashed potatoes (made by a dear friend). Even now, almost two years later, I know mashed potatoes are a way to communicate love to her hurting heart.

When considering tools, it's important to look for coping strategies that are helpful during different stages of grief. One that Amy and I have used the most is a strategy advised by our counselor Mark: *Engaging the Five Senses*. Sometimes this looks like taking a long walk outside, smelling the greenery around you as you walk. Sometimes it's a ride in the car, noticing the buildings that line the road. A favorite song. A special meal. A hands-on project. Engaging your five senses yields autonomy; you are in charge of how you execute this strategy. Figure out what works best for you in those moments of deep grief, when intrusive thoughts fill your mind.

DON'T MISS THE GOD WINKS {AMY}

One of KB's best friends at JSU, Peytan, first introduced Katie Beth to the God Winks concept. Peytan's father, Scott, suffered from a stroke, with consequences that left him mostly wheelchair bound. As her friend, KB took on Peytan's pain as best she could. To this day, Peytan's family still talks about how excited Katie Beth was when Scott took slow steps without his cane after that first and only JSU game she danced in. Peytan and her father were a huge inspiration to Katie Beth. Peytan explained "God Winks" to KB as consistent, small reminders from God that He's in control and that we are not forgotten. They'd often remind each other, Peytan and Katie Beth, that they were each other's reminders. "You're my God Wink," they'd say.

Some might call it coincidence; we call it God Winks. We believe there is no such thing as coincidence. We believe that God is in control. After Katie's accident, we experienced our own God Winks. SQuire Rushnell explains the concept well, in his book *When God Winks*: "When God winks, He is reaffirming that there is absolutely nothing about us that He does not know—our every hurt, our every desire. And that to me is very comforting."[2]

When we were sent a video of a piece of land in Nicaragua where a school named after Katie Beth was to be built *(you'll read about that story a little later)*, it came as no surprise that yellow butterflies circled, dove, and fluttered around the plot and atop the newly planted school sign. See, yellow butterflies had quickly become a surreal symbol that reminded us of Katie Beth. In often unbelievable stories, these butterflies held in their wings both a comfort and a reminder of the joy KB had and left in the lives of those she loved.

In life, Katie had no affinity with butterflies or the color yellow; we didn't even consider the connection until about a week after her accident. The Monday after she passed, we drove to JSU to clean out her apartment. That same day, we attended The Marching Southerners practice, the marching band that The Marching Ballerinas are a vital part of. We wanted to thank them for their support over the course of the past week and wanted to reassure them of the happiness that their team provided Katie Beth with during her time at JSU. At the end of the practice, a wide-eyed flute player came over and introduced herself to our daughter Kimi and me. This young woman was clearly nervous and couldn't offer any justification for what it was she was about to tell us.

"Last week," she said, "after KB's accident, I kept seeing yellow butterflies everywhere. I felt like there was something to it." She handed us her phone. She had taken a picture of a webpage that discussed the significance of yellow butterflies. For centuries, the yellow butterfly has symbolized a myriad of positivities: joy and creativity, happiness and prosperity, as well as hope and excitement. In some cultures, they represent new life and that departed souls are resting peacefully.

We were inspired by her discovery and I shared our discussion with the rest of the family. As it turns out, Jason's mother, Gayle, had a similar encounter. She explained that, on the day of Katie Beth's graveside service, she had watched from afar as Jason, Jacob, Kimi, and I processed as a family. As we left a part of our hearts there with Katie Beth, we slid a flower out of her spray to lay at the base of a family friend's headstone just across the cemetery. As Gayle watched us cross the grass, she noticed a yellow butterfly flying directly behind our path—the same yellow butterfly that she says flew and rested near us as we stood next to Katie Beth's grave. Gayle considered it peculiar at the time, but until this connection was made, she didn't realize its significance.

Coach EK Slaughter, the football coach Katie Beth worked alongside during the 2015 football season, called Jason one evening while we were driving.

"Does Katie have some kind of affection for butterflies?" he asked.

We looked at each other, slightly confused. We hadn't told anybody else about the butterflies. "No," Jason responded, "Why?"

EK explained that he had participated in an adventure race the previous weekend, and became overly exhausted on the last leg of the race.

"I was running and I knew that we had a couple more miles to go, but I was ready to quit," he explained. "Keep in mind, I'd been running through a trail in the woods, but I hadn't seen a lick of wildlife. Right as I hunched over, hands on my knees, about to quit... a yellow butterfly came right past my ear and flew along the path in front of me."

EK quickly tied his thoughts together and told us that in that moment, when the fragile butterfly fluttered past his ear, he instantly thought of Katie Beth. "It's crazy," he laughed, "but I finished. I knew I had to fight through the pain and finish. It was like KB was cheering me on, like she'd done all season."

As if his story wasn't already unbelievable, he continued. Coach Slaughter is one of the lead coaches in the Fellowship of Christian Athletes program at Heritage High School. The evening following his phone call, FCA planned to have baptisms in a large metal tub after football practice. "I'm calling you now from my office," he said. "I set up earlier for the baptismal service, and yellow butterflies came and continually circled around the tank. I'm sitting here now looking out my window at them. That's got to be something."

Quite quickly, we started seeing them more and more, especially when we least expected them. This sign, a yellow butterfly, became what Katie Beth knew as a "God Wink." It was as if God were saying, "Hey, you may feel forgotten, but I see you. You're special. Here, let me show you."

A couple of weeks later, we went to JSU to commemorate Katie Beth by giving each of the Ballerinas a yellow butterfly pin to wear during their routine. It was an overwhelming moment knowing that Katie Beth's presence, one that a few weeks prior had been marching alongside her team with an elated expression, now existed in a way we could only feel. As we were handing them out, a yellow butterfly flew by, catching our attention and reassuring us that our girl was nearer than we realized. When the Ballerinas spread out on the field for their half-time performance, the band began playing and a single yellow butterfly, visible from the stands, danced alongside the Ballerinas.

My friend Dana, who lost her son Daulton in a car accident three weeks after we lost KB, sees images of hearts in unique places (clouds, rocks, etc.). My friend Jamie, who lost her mother, sees God Winks in the form of white feathers. That being said, God Winks come in different shapes and sizes for different people and circumstances. My encouragement to you is to keep your eyes open for God Winks when you're walking through a season of loss, because if you're not watching carefully, you may miss a special reminder from God.

Our encouragement to you is to keep your eyes open and looking in the right direction. Remember to glance back occasionally, look for ways to actively engage the world around you, and keep your eyes open for God Winks. As Charles Spurgeon says, "Wherever Jesus may lead us, he goes before us. If we don't know where we're going, we know with whom we go."

REFLECTION QUESTIONS:

- Have you ever experienced a God Wink? If so, what was it and how did that affect you on your journey?
- What are ways you enjoy looking in the rearview mirror and remembering what's been lost? What are some healthy and purposeful ways to approach this?
- Do you find yourself "sitting in the puddle" at times, unable to live in the present? How does that impact your everyday life (job, family, friends, etc.)? What are some ways to engage your senses to get out of the "puddle"?

CHAPTER IV

LEARN

"All I have seen teaches me to trust the Creator for all
I have not seen."
- Ralph Waldo Emerson

I will instruct you and teach you in the way you should go;
I will counsel you with my loving eye on you.
Psalm 32:8[1]

NAVIGATING THE FOG {JASON}

For months, we had wrestled with the *why* of our loss. Behind closed doors, we demanded that we didn't deserve this. At times, especially early on, it felt like we were the only two, in a world full of happiness and progress, who felt disconnected, isolated, and alone.

At best, we likened this existence to walking through a fog. It felt like anything beyond our noses became heavily opaque, eventually lost in the heaviness of what was before us. We were aware of the fog, but there was nothing we could do to clear it. I'd try to wave it away but it would curl through my fingers, leaving no imprint of my attempt.

About two weeks after the accident, I decided to return to work. I'm a high school teacher and at that time I was also the head coach of our softball team. I felt I needed to get back for my students, players, and partially for myself. Looking back, it was probably too soon. This time in my life was when I was most aware of the fog. One week after the accident, I chose to return to coaching my softball team. Physically I was present for the whole game, but my heart and mind were nowhere to be found. Throughout that night, I would catch myself in a totally different place mentally and emotionally, constantly having to snap myself back to the game that was taking place. I can remember walking through the halls at school, being in the classroom, and interacting with students and adults. But, even in my existence, I felt as if I were a thousand miles away and extremely disconnected, even realizing later that I had no recollection of the content of conversations or situations I was involved in. It was as if everywhere I went and everything I did was an out of body experience. The outside world was moving at its normal breakneck pace and my little world moved in slow motion.

At times, the fog is still deceptively thick, each layer adding to its density. It is simultaneously weightless *and* heavy. Its presence can't be captured, yet it is undeniable. It feels suffocating, yet it's made up of the particles that give us life.

We would love to share with you that this fog has cleared for both Amy and me or that we've been encouraged by others who have experienced loss to understand that it eventually will. Instead, we've discovered that this is the truth: while we are on this earth, the fog will always exist. In times of weariness, it can hover immediately ahead; and on other days, it still remains, but it diffuses and condenses—the fog rests beside us rather than in front of us. Those are the days we want; those are the days we live for.

In explaining the pain we felt from losing Katie, Amy and I later found ourselves explaining the loss to others through the analogy of losing of a limb. As we processed months after the accident, Amy said, "In those first months, the pain was intense and I didn't know how to get out of it, but I knew I had to live. If you lose an arm, you can't constantly focus on the fact that you don't have an arm. You have to keep living, learning how to function without that arm." For me, though, it was different. Without an arm, I felt that the other parts of my body had to be strengthened to make up for that loss. It was as if I couldn't learn from having lost Katie without catering to, and building up, the remaining elements of my life. While I realize it doesn't pan out this way for everyone, in our case, losing Katie deepened my faith and continues to. It has also strengthened mine and Amy's marriage. It's not that one of our perspectives was lacking, it's just that we handled and engaged the responsibility of living differently.

We found ourselves searching for days where the fog was repositioned, but we discovered that God revealed these days to us on His own time. A few months after Katie's accident, our friend Shannon reached out to me about a trip he was leading to Israel. I'd mentioned it to Amy and we quickly agreed that this was an opportunity of a lifetime. When we left, on a trip that was extremely out of character for two school teachers in the middle of the school year, we were pining to play the role of two strangers, to face the pain of losing our beautiful daughter without interruption or intrusion from the world we'd lived in for the past five months. Even still, it took nearly a year for Amy and me to grasp what that trip meant to us. We both experienced moments of clarity, albeit in completely different ways.

Amy feels things differently than I do—she always has. She notices the small things. She also has a knack for sharing her soul and steadily and confidently helping me process the feelings of my own. Amy experienced her moment of visibility first, at the Garden of Gethsemane. While she and I had visited the garden together, my mind was rattled with the fact that this was where Jesus had walked. This space is where He knelt, where His disciples slept, where He prayed and wept. Of course it was overwhelming, but for Amy is was something else.

TAKE THIS CUP FROM ME {AMY}

"Take this cup from me." I'd read and heard Jesus' words plenty of times. I'd read scholars' analyses of Jesus' plea. I knew what it meant, but it wasn't until I visited the Garden of Gethsemane that I truly understood its relevance in my life. Even at my greatest loss, my pain didn't compare to the pain of Christ the hours before his crucifixion.

Luke 22:39-43[2]

39 *He went out and made His way as usual to the Mount of Olives, and the disciples followed Him.* **40** *When He reached the place, He told them, "Pray that you may not enter into temptation."* **41** *Then He withdrew from them about a stone's throw, knelt down, and began to pray,* **42** *"Father, if You are willing, take this cup away from Me—nevertheless, not My will, but Yours, be done."*

43 *Then an angel from heaven appeared to Him, strengthening Him.* **44** *Being in anguish, He prayed more fervently, and His sweat became like drops of blood falling to the ground.*

So many times, I wanted to stop my prayer at "Father, if You are willing, take this cup away from me." I didn't want to give my pain the opportunity to be God's will; I didn't want to utter the rest of Christ's prayer: "not my will, but Yours, be done." Christ did say this, though. Just as He was about to endure God's wrath for sin, the wages of which are death, He submitted to the Father's will. David Platt explains, in his book *Radical*, that this wrath was more than the wrath of one man's sin; it was more than the sin of Jesus' present world. It was the sin of the thousands that had come before Him and the millions who would come after Him.[3]

It was the wrath of sin imposed on Christ for *all* of humanity, *all* of God's children. He took on death, a million times over, because it was the Father's will. The suffering we had experienced the five months leading up to our trip to Israel was, and still is, monumental in our lives. *I don't deserve this,* I thought time and time again. It's a life-altering, faith-challenging, and potentially-pivotal pain, yet it pales in comparison to the suffering of Christ. Like I said, I'd read the words and heard the sermons, but this time, visiting this place, I felt like I understood Jesus' cry a little deeper than before because of what I was living and walking through.

In that same moment, I imagined the weight of God giving His Son, willingly sacrificing His Son, for the sake of others. That resonated with my heart. Having just recently lost my daughter, I couldn't imagine how someone could willingly give up their child, especially, in Christ's case, for people who may or may not receive the gift of Christ's sacrifice.

Platt puts it eloquently, "In that holy moment, all the righteous wrath and justice of God due us came rushing down like a torrent on Christ himself. Some say, 'God looked down and could not bear to see the suffering that the soldiers were inflicting on Jesus, so he turned away.' But this is not true. God turned away because he could not bear to see your sin and my sin on his Son."[3] In a similar way to our salvation through Christ's sacrifice, Katie Beth's death ultimately yielded development in a city that is now so close to our heart: Tomás Borge, Nicaragua. For years, students will enter the school's doors and possibly never know about our daughter. Maybe they'll be taught in a classroom and never truly accept the Jesus that our Katie loved so dearly. But, because of Katie's death, because of what God chose to do with Katie's life, a lasting impact exists. Most of the time, that's no consolation. From an earthly perspective, it doesn't make me feel any better about having lost our daughter. From an eternal perspective, a perspective likely to never be understood from this side of heaven, I have hope.

Genesis 1:26 tells us that we are made in the image of God. Yet, so often, we believe the lie that God doesn't understand us. We believe that He is somehow disconnected from us, His creation, so carefully crafted to be His image bearers. When we weep, grieve, and hurt, we forget that He has too.

Genesis 1:26-27[4]

26 *Then God said, "Let Us make man in Our image, according to Our likeness. They will rule the fish of the sea, the birds of the sky, the livestock, all the earth, and the creatures that crawl on the earth."*
27 *So God created man in His own image;*
He created him in the image of God;
He created them male and female.

The question is: do we control our God-given emotions or do we allow them to control us? When considering our salvation through Jesus Christ, imagine if God had chosen to react in the same way we may have. Imagine if we so delicately created something, asked it only to live and love what we had created for it, and it deliberately disobeyed. Imagine the betrayal, the hurt, and the anger that we'd feel. What would you do? Would you lower yourself, the creator, to be restricted to the body you designed for something else? Would you sacrifice yourself to be reconciled with the one thing that you created that turned away from you? Probably not. Yet, He chose to love us, unconditionally, despite our disobedience, denial, and rejection.

God didn't give us these emotions for some random reason. These emotions are a part of His heart, too. When we are afraid to own our emotions, we need to remember that they come from God, because we are made in His image. It's a hard concept to grasp, but when we felt the excruciating pain of losing something that was, and is, one of our most precious purposes, God felt that with us. When we were overjoyed, just a few weeks prior, watching Katie Beth glow with delight as a part of The Marching Ballerinas, God felt that too. When we have days where it feels like just existing is a chore, God has felt that too. I feel this way, but so has He. And it's okay. Because he understands you, allow God to teach you; He will.

ENCOUNTERING CHRIST {JASON}

I now know Amy's feeling all too well. We committed to calling out Satan on his lies of isolation, but that certainly didn't stop us from feeling the weight of the loss we so desperately wished God would have manifested differently. As these realizations unfolded, we continually asked God, and sometimes still do, why we had to lose our daughter just to understand Christ's redemptive character.

A few days before, we had taken a tour of Magdala. Our tour guide, Jane told us that there had been plans to build a women's center along the Sea of Galilee a few years back. As Amy and I walked hand in hand toward our destination, I remember listening as Jane explained that the women's center couldn't be built on the land we were approaching because laser imaging had discovered a first century synagogue, later determined to be the city of Magdala. All along the Sea of Galilee rested several synagogues, synagogues in which the New Testament tells us Jesus did His ministry. The feeling of walking where Jesus walked, having a conversation where Jesus spoke, eating where Jesus had fed thousands—it was all so surreal. This synagogue, though, in the newly unearthed Magdala, will always hold a special place in my heart.

Magdala of old, also known as *Migdal Nunaiya*, translates to "tower of fish," aptly named after its fish industry and preservation. While the ancient city now lay in ruins, its sister city, the modern day Migdal, sits just east of the ancient city, borrowing again from the Hebrew word meaning "tower." It's no coincidence, then, that this site in Israel served as a sort of light tower for Amy and me. We didn't understand the *why* then, and we often still question it. But instead of "wallowing in the why," as Amy says, we hold to the truths that we first experienced during our time in Israel. Faith transformed from a distant concept to a desperate necessity—a true means of survival.

In the port city, the Encounter Chapel rests just below the larger main chapel, built out of the original stone that lined the market place. Just above the re-crafted stone benches, artist Daniel Coriola brought to life a miracle often overlooked in scripture. This space was so intimate and Coriola's work was one of many focal points in this room. Just beyond the altar, on the wall, are Jesus' feet scrambling through a Magdalian crowd. Amidst the chaos of the painting, a woman's hand reaches out of her cloak barely grazing Jesus' robe, right above his brown sandals. Where her finger meets a tassel from his garment, a discreet light shines.

Even though I could only see these figures from the ankle down, I knew the story. Until then, though, I hadn't visualized it in application to my own life. There, even if just for a brief moment, is where the fog, which had been so heavily settled in front of me, began to illuminate. Looking back, it was as if I became small. It wasn't that my problems, or my family's loss were considerably "less than," but my experience standing in front of that painting rawly exposed my brokenness against a tapestry of humanity's existence—an existence riddled with sin and pain. It exposed a desperate need for someone like Christ.

Luke 8:40-48[5]

40 *When Jesus returned, the crowd welcomed Him, for they were all expecting Him.* **41** *Just then, a man named Jairus came. He was a leader of the synagogue. He fell down at Jesus' feet and pleaded with Him to come to his house,* **42** *because he had an only daughter about 12 years old, and she was at death's door. While He was going, the crowds were nearly crushing Him.* **43** *A woman suffering from bleeding for 12 years, who had spent all she had on doctors yet could not be healed by any,* **44** *approached from behind and touched the tassel of His robe. Instantly her bleeding stopped.*
45 *"Who touched Me?" Jesus asked.*
When they all denied it, Peter said, "Master, the crowds are hemming You in and pressing against You."
46 *"Someone did touch Me," said Jesus. "I know that power has gone out from Me."* **47** *When the woman saw that she was discovered, she came trembling and fell down before Him. In the presence of all the people, she declared the reason she had touched Him and how she was instantly cured.* **48** *"Daughter,"* *He said to her, "your faith has made you well. Go in peace."*

A woman who had lost all hope, a woman who was slowly decaying inside, who was hurting and alone—she reached out. She reached for the smallest thread, anything to get her closer to Jesus, the Man she knew could heal. We have no knowledge that she had seen or heard about the miracles of Jesus; therefore, we can't assume that her faith was founded only on these things. Instead, she was desperate for healing and confident in who Christ said He was.

I've since grown to understand that we'll never be completely healed of our pain on Earth. Our hearts will always be broken, yet God's heart is for those who long for healing. There, on the streets surrounding that chapel, Jesus radically transformed a life. I'm as broken, as unclean, as desperate, and as longing as the sick woman who reached for The Rabbi. There we were, in this place, where Christ bestowed his mercy and healed her internal bleeding, eradicating the shame and uncleanliness that accompanied it. I desperately wanted this same miracle. I wanted Jesus to heal my broken heart so that I could live more wholly.

We all silently observed the painting for a few minutes, and as we were about to leave, Shannon stopped the group. Because Shannon was a family friend, he and his wife were aware of our loss, as were some of the other travelers in the group. Some of them were bearing their own pain as well. He said, "I don't think we can walk away from here, being a place where healing has taken place, and not spend some time asking God for healing in the broken places in our lives. If you need that now, this is your time." At that moment, I didn't experience a fainting flood of emotion, but an undeniable presence of God. I'd asked why for months and I often still do, but in that room, I came face to face with God and I was reminded of His faithful presence, His understanding, and His heart. I had been reaching through a thick fog for something, perhaps something as small as His robe's tassel, for something tangible, something to purify my pain. In this glimpse of clarity, I affirmed that God was still good. He was with me.

The traps of deception, intrusive thought, and *what if* still lay scattered throughout our daily path. To avoid the crippling pain these mental states could cause, and because life didn't seem to stop for us, we learned to continually profess this: "God, You are still good."

God, You're still good. It didn't roll eloquently off the tongue; in fact, for me, it was often said through gritted teeth, in agonizing pain.

I've often thought about those who experience loss without being able to believe these words and I can't imagine their hurt—simply because, at times, it was the only thing that enabled me to put one foot in front of the other. He hurts with us. He wants to bring fullness to us. We are not alone. *You* are not alone.

(RE)POSITIONING {BOTH}

We are educators and both of us hold multiple college degrees, therefore learning is something we understand and can relate to. In our experience in the classroom, we find that our students learn best when they position themselves to do so. Whether that is coming in for tutoring, committing to practicing a song after school (Amy is a music/drama teacher), asking questions, or simply staying engaged during class, their conscientious decisions to progress improve their ability to glean the most from what we desire to teach them. It has been no different for us during our grief journey. We have chosen to position ourselves in the hopes of learning from the Father all that He desires to teach us. We've done this through seeking counseling, serving others, and traveling to Israel, just to name a few strategies.

Re-positioning yourself, post-loss, doesn't have to look like traveling to a far off place or doing something "grand." It's more about having eyes to see and ears to hear what's happening around you *(refer back to chapters 2 & 3)*. Maybe God wants to teach you something as you're mowing the grass or cleaning your house. He may have something for you to learn through a relationship with a co-worker or while comforting a friend during their pain. But then again, maybe an opportunity presents itself, that doesn't seem to even relate to your situation, that God wants to use to teach you something about your pain in order to bring redemption to your loss. He wants to teach you something that will alter your perspective and could change the trajectory of your journey. Don't miss it, and more importantly, don't *dismiss* it. There's always an opportunity to learn, if you're willing.

REFLECTION QUESTIONS:

- How does viewing your pain through the lens of Jesus' sacrifice, and God accomplishing his will through it, change your perspective about your loss?

- Have you experienced a "Magdala moment"? What did that look like and what was God saying to you through it?

- As you reflect on your loss(es), what have you learned along the way that you should revisit periodically? What do you possibly need to do in order to be more aware of what God is trying to teach you?

Clockwise from above: Carter Family Photo 2016, One of our favorite senior pictures of Katie Beth (photo credit to Michelle McKibben), Katie Beth dancing at the JSU home opener on September 1, 2016. This would be her first and only time dancing as a Marching Ballerina at a game. (photo credit to Mark Dupont), Peytan, Shea, and Katie Beth with Scott Dill the night he walked without his cane, The last picture taken of Katie Beth moments before leaving our house on September 5, 2016.

Clockwise from top left: This shot from Katie Beth's senior pictures captures her laugh and fun loving spirit and how we picture her in heaven (photo credit to Michelle McKibben), Standing with our extended family in front of Katie Beth Carter Memorial Institute in Tomas Borge, Nicaragua. February 2018, Jason and Amy on the Mount of Olives overlooking Jerusalem, Daniel Coriola's painting "Encounter" at Magdala in the Encounter Chapel (photo credit to Judy Hays), Jason and Amy praying over Katie Beth Carter Memorial Institute on their first trip to Nicaragua. February 2018

CHAPTER V

LIVE

"Never be afraid to trust an unknown future
to a known God."

- Corrie Ten Boom

A thief comes only to steal and to kill and to destroy.
I have come so that they may have life and have it
in abundance.

John 10:10[1]

{AMY}

In the initial aftermath of the loss, I don't remember much. I know now why the words "survived by" are used in obituaries, because those first few days and weeks are merely survival. I remember my friend Carolee reminding me to "just breathe." It's really all I could do. For days, I didn't eat or sleep. I couldn't have even if I'd wanted to. I was just breathing. How was I supposed to make funeral arrangements for my child? It didn't feel natural. It wasn't right.

The pendulum eventually shifted and I wanted to sleep all the time because it was a brief respite from the intense pain. Nighttime was hard because my mind would race with persistent, desperate thoughts. *What exactly happened? Why, God, why? Will I dream of her tonight? Lord, take me to heaven in my sleep so I can be with you and KB!* I longed to see her, touch her, and talk to her, even if in a dream. Eventually the medication would kick in, and I would drift off to sleep on my tear-stained pillow. Morning certainly wasn't any easier, I'd wake up disappointed that I hadn't been able to dream and see my sweet Katie Beth. Each morning, I also had to face the reality that this horrible tragedy wasn't just a bad dream. This was my "new normal," a phrase I still absolutely hate. How on earth is *this* normal in any way?

I went through a season where I didn't really want to live anymore. I just wanted the pain to end. I wasn't contemplating suicide, or anything of the sort, but my desperation to be with Katie Beth again outweighed my drive to function otherwise. Heaven, with my daughter, truly sounded so much better. Even now, my heart longs for her and I ache to be with her. I know that day will come; every day is one day closer to that sweet reunion. At some point, I came to terms with the fact that God has more for me to accomplish in this life. Simply put, there's a reason I'm still here.

If you are walking through loss and you ever reach a point of utter hopelessness, *please* reach out to someone, *anyone*, for help. I can't emphasize this enough! I understand the feeling of overwhelming pain, but I also know that taking your life is *never* the answer to that suffering. If anything, that will only perpetuate greater pain and suffering in the hearts and lives of those who love you and want to help you heal.

Let me also say, there is NO SHAME in needing medicine to help you live well. I was already taking a mild anxiety prescription prior to Katie's accident, and then was placed on additional medication for several months following. I was battling intense chest pains, especially at night. Although I knew this was most likely anxiety related, I wasn't able to manage it with prayer or mindfulness. In some cases, the "church" has led people to believe that their faith should be great enough to negate the *need* for medication in order to navigate life. Now, don't get me wrong, I am not promoting unnecessary or abused drug use for the purpose of "numbing the pain." Pain demands to be felt and addressed, but there are times that proper medical intervention is needed to help with chemical imbalances or paralyzing anxiety. Just as my diabetic father needs his insulin to live a healthier life, I need my mild anxiety medication to live a fuller life. My medical need for a prescription is not a reflection of my faith, or lack thereof. I do think it is important to find what works best for you. I know, at one point, a particular medicine the doctor prescribed for me to take after KB's accident was causing my depression to worsen.

There were days when I literally could not get out of bed. I would just sleep, wake up and cry, and then go back to sleep. Then there were days where I would somehow manage to make it out of bed, but soon found myself weeping uncontrollably on the floor. These were the darkest days of my grief journey. The sorrow was indeed overwhelming, but I also believe that particular medicine I was on was making matters worse. Luckily, I was able to recognize this and seek other treatment options from my doctor. It is important to find what works for you and to have a doctor who is cooperative and intentional in finding the best possible solution for you.

We must recognize we are comprised of mind, body, and spirit, and it is important to steward each of those well as we walk through life. Take care of yourself physically, emotionally, and spiritually. Look for ways to strengthen these areas. Do what you need to do, for *you*, to be able to live well and love well.

A PICTURE FROM THE FATHER

Over my twenty year teaching career, I've directed and produced many musical theater productions. Because of this, I've developed a keen sense of visualizing what a scene or show should look like, and how to create those images on stage. God created my mind to work this way, and He occasionally speaks to me through visual images. A few years ago, before Katie's accident, God gave me a vision that I was this warrior princess standing in the middle of a battlefield, where a war had obviously been fought. I was surrounded by death and the land had been decimated by fire. Destruction and chaos were all around me, much like a movie scene. I witnessed great loss and damage, but it was clear that the battle was already over. I limped up to the King, broken and battered, and he said to me, "Well done, my good and faithful servant!"

This image, one that reflected life as a child of God, wasn't a picture of me in a beautiful white dress, twirling or dancing through fields of flowers. It was a picture of fighting a brutal battle, and remembering that *"for our battle is not against flesh and blood, but against the rulers, against the authorities, against the world powers of this darkness, against the spiritual forces of evil in the heavens."* **(Ephesians 6:12[2]).**

We have an enemy, and he is out to destroy us. He is very real and we must be prepared for battle. I don't think I realized just how intense the war would become. We know how the story ends, though. With Christ, we have hope and victory will come. Day by day, sometimes moment by moment, we must choose to live, to fight the good fight, and trust that God *will* be victorious.

MAKING GOALS {JASON}

I've considered that God sees things in a multidimensional state. We see things three dimensionally, only recognizing what is in front of us, and only viewing things that interact with our life. He, however, sees throughout all time and space that has ever existed. He sees all the moving parts, when we just see *our* moving parts. Knowing this, I've accepted that there's a bigger story. I can have peace that my life, and Katie Beth's life, is not just about my family's story.

John Eldredge sheds light on this concept, in the prologue of his book *Epic: The Story God is Telling and the Role That is Yours to Play*: "What if all great stories that have ever moved you—what if they are all telling you something about the true Story into which you were born, the Epic into which you have been cast?" he asks. "We won't begin to understand our lives or what this so-called gospel is that Christianity speaks of, until we understand the Story in which we have found ourselves. For when you were born, you were born into an Epic that has already been under way for quite some time. It is a Story of beauty and intimacy and adventure, a Story of danger and loss and heroism and betrayal."[3] In essence, Eldredge challenges us to consider our unique roles in the greater Story that is God's will.

The uniqueness that inhabits us exists because that's how God created us to be. That being said, our goals and God's plan coincide within our hearts. These goals develop from the desires in our heart, but don't necessarily always come to fruition. The problem and confusion surfaces when we make goals and immediately expect to see their completion or effect. When we expect God to use the desires He placed in our hearts *our* way, on *our* time, we experience a collision between these goals and God's plan.

Philippians 3:7-11[4]

7 *But everything that was a gain to me, I have considered to be a loss because of Christ.*

8 *More than that, I also consider everything to be a loss in view of the surpassing value of knowing Christ Jesus my Lord. Because of Him I have suffered the loss of all things and consider them filth, so that I may gain Christ* 9 *and be found in Him, not having a righteousness of my own from the law, but one that is through faith in Christ—the righteousness from God based on faith.* 10 *My goal is to know Him and the power of His resurrection and the fellowship of His sufferings, being conformed to His death,* 11 *assuming that I will somehow reach the resurrection from among the dead.*

In Philippians, Paul reminds us that loss is worth gaining Christ. Paul shows us that becoming more like Christ means participating in His sufferings. In this passage, he expresses to the church of Philippi that the things he's endured for their sake are all beneficial, because these sufferings allow him to walk in humility, like Jesus.

Tragic circumstances have the unique ability to bring us to a place of humility. It would have been so easy for Paul to live in self-pity—the man was beaten, imprisoned, and broken—but he continued to embrace his suffering. Striving to maintain a mindset like Paul's has brought me closer to the Lord than I've ever been. I've certainly had my days of sulking, and do from time to time, but I'm currently in the process of committing my loss to

Christ, to grow His Kingdom while I become more like Him.

LIVING FULLY

> *If we found out that the world was going to end on Tuesday*
> *morning what would everybody do? It's funny how the thought*
> *of that can make some things real important and a lot of things*
> *seem pretty worthless too.*
>
> *- Ben Rector, "Like the World is Going to End"*

Having an end-of-the-world or eternal mindset definitely gives us a different perspective on what's important in life. Many times, an event in our lives can cause us to step back and reevaluate what truly holds significant value.

We knew when we lost Katie Beth that our life would never be the same. We have, and still have, a lot of questions. This has easily been a journey with a lot of questions and a lot of struggle—generally and spiritually. During this journey, we've been challenged to further establish what we believe and to fully rely on God in those moments. So far, this journey of loss has caused Amy and me to learn more at every step. One of the things I have come to realize is that our random pain, struggle, or tragedy may not always be as random, erratic, or as meaningless as we think—or at least not as void of purpose as we feel. If I had to boil it down, I'd say that there are three things I've learned about pain and loss in regards to living fully: to trust Him with my story, to live in the now, and to maintain the proper perspective.

Trust Him with Your Story

Trust Him with your story because He makes your story matter. Let's take Joseph's life, in Genesis 37-50, as an example. Joseph's story demonstrates that God is in control, even when it is not obvious in our immediate circumstances. Joseph's circumstance was unimaginable—he was thrown in a pit and betrayed by his brothers, sold into slavery, and imprisoned—yet he still chose to submit to the promises of God. Nearly fifteen years later, the tables had turned, and he served his brothers, those who had betrayed him, from his position at Pharaoh's palace. Not once in scripture do we see Joseph question the promises or plans of God. In fact, the scripture continually states that "The Lord was with Joseph." Because of his faith and unwavering spirit, I believe Joseph knew that God was at work in his circumstances.

Joseph trusted God with his story. He had no idea that his suffering fit into a larger plot, one that involved millions of people and centuries of history. His life, and ours, is not simply a succession of isolated events, randomly strung together, but a story with a purpose that we may not see and will never entirely understand. Now that history has unfolded, we know that Joseph moved his family to Egypt, saved what would become the nation of Israel who eventually became slaves who were led to freedom by Moses. This seemingly insignificant group would turn into a mighty people that led us all the way to Jesus. In the face of evil and turmoil, Joseph believed in God's transcendent purpose and that God's grace had triumphed over it.

I can't begin to know or even imagine how the loss of my daughter, and my response to that, will impact the lives of people long after I'm gone. My struggle is probably much like Joseph's was. There are days I'm sitting in my own prison of sorts that I didn't create nor did I do anything to deserve, yet I still have a choice as to what I will do with my story. Will I trust that God really does have a larger plan and purpose or will I hold on to it trying to manipulate the outcome? I've come to realize I can't redeem the loss of Katie Beth no matter how hard I try, no matter what I do. The only hope I have of redemption is loosening my grip, realizing my story isn't over, and trusting the Father with it.

Live in the Now

To avoid missing the moments of the present, commit to living in the now. Amy and I will be the first to admit that we are not perfect at subscribing to this motto; however, we decided early on that we would live as fully as we could. In order to do this, I had to commit to the present, not to time.

One of my favorite books comes from the *Lord of the Rings* trilogy, *The*

Fellowship of the Ring by J.R.R. Tolkien. In it, Frodo recalls his devastating circumstance and says to Gandalf, "I wish it need not have happened in my time." Gandalf, known for his wisdom, responds by saying, "So do all who live to see such times, but that is not for them to decide. All we have to decide is what to do with the time that is given us."[5]

Before Katie's accident, I wore a watch every day. Now, I wear a watch, but it has no working parts. On its face, instead of ticking hands and grooved dials, the word "Now" reminds me of what is truly important. There are times throughout my day when I will look down out of habit to check the time and see the three large letters N-O-W staring back at me. It's such a strong reminder that time truly is fleeting and what matters most are the moments in the present. I don't want to miss the moments that God places in front of me, whether they be with my wife, with my kids, or anything else. I want to keep my eyes open and ears attentive to what He's doing around me. Your pain, your suffering, and your circumstance has much more to do with what He's doing *in* and *through* you than what is happening *to* you.

Maintain the Proper Perspective

At the beginning of this process, my question to God was this, "God, you say you're good and that you're for me. You say you're sovereign, yet my eighteen year old daughter, who loved you with all of her heart, is dead. How does that work?"

After asking a lot of hard questions why and being angry for two months, God finally gave me an answer to my question: *"You live in a broken world and not even My children are immune to pain and suffering. But I am good and I am for you. And my promises are still true. You just live in a broken world."* If I'm honest, I didn't particularly like this answer, but it was an answer nonetheless. It didn't take away the pain or even the questions I had at times, but it began to help me gain God's perspective rather than my own worldly perspective. Up to this point, I couldn't and wouldn't sing those lyrics that Kimi had sung on the way to Atlanta. I questioned His goodness and I surely didn't believe He was "perfect in all of His ways." But because His answer came as a loving, compassionate Father, not as a reprimand, coupled with the fact that my 15 year old daughter could believe in His character in her darkest moment, my heart began to shift. This was the moment that started the process that eventually enabled me to choose to believe that He *is* good and He *is* for me and that His promises *are* true, even if they don't *feel* true. I still struggle with this some days, but I'm beginning to rest in this truth. This belief allows me to find purpose in the pain.

Have eyes to see: gain and keep the proper perspective. Instead of asking "Why me?" try asking "Why not me?" for a change. Why do we think we should escape heartache and pain and struggle? If Jesus, our example, endured suffering, why would we think we are exempt?

Psalm 103:7[6]

He (God) made known his ways to Moses, his deeds to the people of Israel.

The time period this passage is referencing is that in which Moses was leading Israel in the desert. The children of Israel only saw *what God did*, but Moses *understood why God did it*. Knowledge and perspective are similar, but not the same concept. Knowledge is simply knowing or learning what God has said and done. Perspective, however, is understanding why He said and did it. This answers the *why* questions of life. Why wouldn't we desire this? Who wouldn't want to better understand the *whys* of life? After all, perspective is not what we see, but the way we see it.

Like the rest of us who have suffered great pain, Joseph would have never chosen his story and definitely couldn't have predicted the outcome or have completely understood the implications of it. However, at the end of the book in Genesis 50, Jacob, Joseph's father, dies and his brothers are fearful of their future as slaves to Joseph, the brother they had once betrayed. In verse 19-20, Joseph encourages them:

Genesis 50:19-20[7]

19 Don't be afraid. Am I in the place of God? 20 You intended to harm me, but God intended it for good to accomplish what is now being done, the saving of many lives.

Joseph didn't miss the moment; he saw an opportunity to show his brothers grace. Think about that! What if Joseph chose to be bitter and angry? What if he wallowed in his incredibly dismal circumstances? If he had, it's unlikely that he would have landed in the palace as Prime Minister, a savior to a whole nation.

Who knows what's at stake when it comes to our situations? How will our response impact the lives, and possibly the eternity, of others? *Trust Him with Your story*; be faithful in the place you find yourself because your story matters. Don't miss the moments; live in the now. Don't get so caught up in where you've been or where you're going that you miss what God is up to right now. Gain the proper perspective; ask God *what?* instead of *why?*

God, what are you up to?

God, what do you want me to see?

God, what are you wanting to do in me?

God, what are you wanting to do in others through my situation or circumstance?

REFLECTION QUESTIONS:

- In what ways have you been made more like Christ through your pain? In what ways do you need to entrust Him with your story?

- What's important right now in your life? What are the areas in your life where you don't want to miss the moments? Write them down and make it a matter of prayer. Put it on your mirror, in your car, at your desk, or somewhere you can see it every day.

- How do you need to shift your perspective concerning your loss/ circumstances? What may God be up to in your situation? How can your pain impact or minister to others?

CHAPTER VI

LOVE

"I used to think I needed all the answers,
I used to need to know that I was right,
I used to be afraid of things
I couldn't cover up in black and white.
But I just wanna look more like love,
I just wanna look more like love.
This whole world is spinning crazy, I can't quite keep up.
It's the one thing around here
that we don't have quite enough of,
So I just wanna look a little more like love."
- Ben Rector, "More Like Love"

Do everything in love.
1 Corinthians 16:14[1]

FOR THE COMFORTER {JASON}

If you're a bereaved parent, sibling, or friend, or a victim of abuse, rape, or harassment, or have experienced a myriad of other tragedies in life, you absolutely deserve to be heard. You need counsel, whether professionally in an office or casually over a cup of coffee. Whether through spiritual, communal, medical or a combination of all measures, take care of yourself. Once you've begun that process, once you feel stable and able to give back, consider taking care of others as well. We have an obligation to be available and present for those who are walking the path after us.

However, being empathetic can be daunting, especially when it challenges the pursuer to reflect and relive hard times. Just because you can relate doesn't mean you have to. In the same way, just because you don't know what to say doesn't mean you need to stay away.

Amy and I are both huge fans of John and Stasi Eldredge. Their works, prior to and after Katie's death, have been grand inspirations to us on our spiritual walk. Just recently, John and his colleagues at Ransomed Heart conducted a segment on their podcast series, called "Consecrating Empathy." In the segment, John recognizes that being empathetic, especially as Christians, can be incredibly overwhelming. Since we live in a system that offers mass media and circulation, it's simply difficult to avoid the heartbreak the world faces every day. The call for empathic believers isn't to address all of the world's heartache, to dwell only on positive thoughts about the world, or to avoid the world's pain; instead, we successfully give of ourselves, our experiences, and our love through consecrating our gifts to God.[2]

> **Romans 12:1-2[3]**
>
> **1** *Therefore, brothers, by the mercies of God, I urge you to present your bodies as a living sacrifice, holy and pleasing to God; this is your spiritual worship.* **2** *Do not be conformed to this age, but be transformed by the renewing of your mind, so that you may discern what is the good, pleasing, and perfect will of God.*

Eldredge explains that empathy, like any gift, is in collision with several other forces pulling at our lives. Consecrating this gift to God is aligning it with Jesus. It's not only asking Jesus *how* to use our compassion, but asking him *what* we should be empathetic about. When we think about it like this, we recognize that supporting others, especially those Christ has drawn us to, is an act of service with a dual role, both to man and to God.

Be Available

Having walked the road of losing a child, we have a sickeningly deep anguish for those who have experienced this type of loss, or who will. For example, eight years before Katie's death, we walked through loss with some close family friends of ours, Doug and Carolee, who lost their 22 year old son, Michael. For the first five days after they had received the news of the incident, we stayed at their house with them. We didn't know what to do and we couldn't even begin to understand their hurt. They told us that they needed us to help them get everything in order and we did exactly that. With an unexpected funeral around the corner, we helped with the painful logistics that were likely to be a blur to them. Our method of offering emotional support was simply being present. We didn't attempt to connect in a way that we knew we couldn't. I remember laying in the recliner in Doug and Carolee's living room and knowing that I couldn't even imagine what they were going through.

For years, Doug experienced intense anxiety and panic after the loss of his son. For reasons I couldn't understand at the time, Doug regularly lived as if his son had just passed and I'll forever regret any time I had secretly questioned his anxiety, uncertainty, and weariness. I simply couldn't understand. Now, ten years later, I still wake up and feel like what happened to Katie two years ago actually happened yesterday. Other days, it feels miles away and the guilt hits for feeling as though I'm "moving on," which of course is an unrealistic concept.

We had comforted them during their time of loss, and when we were walking that same road, they were comforting us. Carolee offered us a piece of advice, "You'll never get over it, but you will get through it." At times, we questioned if we *could* get through it. Though we are getting through it, Carolee was absolutely correct in saying that we will never get over it.

An old acquaintance recently lost their teenage son in a car accident. Because we knew them, and because Amy and I related on some level to their pain, we reached out to them individually. After a few sentences offering our presence and our support through social media, all we received in return was "Thank you" from the father. This seemed short, but we understood that their loss was not about us. Offering condolences should only be about being present, being available, and loving those who are hurting and hurting with them.

Amy also reached out to the mother of the child, "So sorry to hear of your loss... it's hell, pure hell. We are praying and we are here. Send a message if you need someone to talk to." Within a few hours, she had responded with a lengthy message letting Amy know that she was comforted in knowing that someone could relate and be a listening ear. That being said, don't offer to be a listening ear if all you'll do is talk. Those who have meant the most to us in this process have simply been present and listened.

Simply loving people has healing qualities, emotionally and physically. Genuinely loving others not only helps the person being loved, but it actually brings healing to the giver of that love. Amy and I can truly say that we have experienced this firsthand. Losing Katie Beth has opened our eyes and hearts to the the pain of others who have lost children, which has enabled us to show deep compassion and love others in ways we never could have before. This process has healed broken places in us and given us the strength to continue on this journey.

Carefully Connect

If you've lost something, nothing is to be negated from this discussion of the pain and growth that comes from loss. Losing a pet and losing a child are two different things, yet they both have potential to yield great sorrow, just as losing a job and losing a limb and hearing "It's cancer" versus "We have to let you go" are two entirely different situations. Just because you've lost something does not mean that you can relate with someone who has lost something else. All loss is hard. It's not a less than greater than game;

however, it is a game of difference. Loss is not comparable.

To one person, something may seem devastating, while it may seem minor to another. Everybody has their cross to bear. Even considering our heartache, we live a comfortable life. We aren't rich, but we certainly are compared to some people in the world. As difficult as our journey has been, we've visited places where people lose children regularly. I can't imagine losing another child, but I certainly can't imagine living in conditions that nearly guarantee that I will.

Just recently, my cousin Paul lost his daughter Sarah who was twelve years old. After she'd been in the bathroom for a while, Paul went to check on her. When Sarah didn't answer, Paul opened the door to find his daughter, lifeless and blue, lying in the tub. Sarah had a grand mal seizure while taking a bath. Since her death, Paul has questioned himself, constantly asking the *what ifs*. Of course, Amy and I have lost Katie, but we cannot relate to the same pain Paul and his wife, Nancy, feel. We had the choice as to whether or not to see Katie's body post-accident. Advised by the emergency room doctor, we chose not to. Our last image was of our daughter, laughing her loud, deep laugh, at a family game night. Though both of our families lost something precious, each of our experiences is unique.

Every loss is so incredibly intimate and personal. This doesn't mean that you should keep your mouth shut, step away from the situation, or feel uncomfortable. But, it does mean that you should take into consideration that someone else's loss is not an avenue for you to obligatorily connect. Instead, it's an opportunity to be present and to listen. Over-relating, even when well intentioned, comes across as a self-centered action. Someone's loss is about them. Don't make it about you. Understand that you do not have to offer advice. You do not have to connect the death of someone's son to the death of your cat. In fact, it's probably in your best interest not to. Just be present and love them where they are.

Say Something

If you've heard me say that you're better off saying nothing, you've misunderstood. No, it's absolutely not best for you to say nothing to a person who has experienced loss. Whether or not it's what you mean, not saying anything translates that you're uncomfortable and that you don't know what to do. *Nothing* is not helpful. Acknowledge to yourself that the solution is out of your control. For your loved one, acknowledge the fact that you don't know what to do or say. Show them that you're equally as lost, but that you are present for them, however that may look.

The best example I can provide of the quiet comfort of a friend's presence happened at our home, during the days following the accident. Our friends, Tim and Wally, served us in an unforgettable way. Upon entering the room crowded with familiar faces, they pulled me aside and simply said, "Hey, We're here. We'll be here until it's all over. Don't worry about entertaining us or anyone else. We'll be the ones that ask everyone to leave whenever you two are ready to have an empty house. Whatever you need, just let us know."

Throughout the evening, people came to love and care for us. At times this was overwhelming because we were at a loss for words; other times, there was intense comfort in the presence of an understanding parent, close family member, or friend who had travelled just to grieve with us. Throughout the evening, what I remember the most, was glancing around the room to see Wally or Tim chatting with a visitor. People came and went, all appreciated, but Tim and Wally were out of the way and present— available to do anything we asked of them, even if that meant spending their evening in a corner chair. Something about their presence spoke volumes to me. Presence is all I needed at the time.

LIVING IN FEAR

My cousin Paul called me a few weeks after losing Sarah. "I've lost half of what I have," he said, explaining that Sarah and his wife Nancy were the two most important things in his life. He explained that, because he lost Sarah so suddenly, he feared the same situation would happen with Nancy. "You have another daughter, Jason. How do you keep your faith knowing that the same thing could happen to Kimi?"

I'd contemplated this a million times before he even asked this question, yet I still didn't have a good answer. "If there's been a struggle outside of losing Katie Beth, keeping the faith has been it," I said. "Every time Kimi steps in a car or travels, I just have to come to grips with the fact that I'm not guaranteed that she'll be safe a hundred percent of the time."

The reality of this hit me within a week or so of Katie's accident. Kimi had asked to go hiking with a friend for a change of scenery outside of the house. We agreed and gave her a time to be home. When she hadn't arrived at the agreed upon time, I called her to no avail. I called several times and it went to voicemail. Not wanting to cause Amy to panic, I stepped outside and Jacob followed. At this point, my heart was racing and a dozen scenarios went through my head as to why she wasn't answering; none of them good. Jacob and I continued this process for what seemed like an eternity, though it probably was just a handful of minutes. In those moments, all the feelings and emotions I had felt the day I received the call about Katie Beth came flooding in like a raging river... fear, hopelessness, anger, panic, weakness, sorrow. Needless to say, when she finally called Jacob, they had a heart to heart about punctuality and communication.

Since then, there have been several times fear has reared its ugly head as Kimi drives out of the driveway to go somewhere or is on her way home. I would love to say it goes away or it's an easy fix, but that would be a lie. The truth is that it is just a part of the journey we are on, and we are learning how to navigate that piece of the road. When those feelings rise up, I typically find an activity to keep my mind from wandering into dark places, whether that's mowing the grass, tinkering in the garage, or washing dishes. This is one of those areas where it is of crucial importance to recognize you can't walk it alone. Amy has been strong and steady in these moments, knowing exactly what to say and how to ease my fear. By myself, it is very likely that the fear would be too overwhelming.

Coming to the realization that loss could come knocking at the door again is not an easy pill to swallow. God loves Sarah and Katie Beth just as much as He loves Kimi and Jacob. I could lose another child, but I have to trust that He is for me, that He is good, and that He's proven to be nothing but faithful in my life through this process. I trust His heart and I've seen the evidence of His faithfulness.

I John 4:8[4]

There is no fear in love, but perfect love casts out fear.

LET YOURSELF LOVE AGAIN {AMY}

Just two days after losing Katie Beth, we were being bombarded with lots of food, friends, and special deliveries. That evening though, we noticed people passing by the front window of our home. We walked outside to find a special group of friends (and their children) had come over to do a prayer walk around our home. They didn't come to "visit", they simply came to cover us with prayer. We know there were many people who prayed for us during that time, but we will *always* remember and cherish those special prayer warriors who came and encircled our home that night. The very next day was Katie's service, and we needed all the love and prayers offered up to help us face that moment.

Alfred Lord Tennyson said, "'Tis better to have loved and lost than never to have loved at all." Those are easy words to quote if you've never lost someone you loved so deeply, someone who was once in your womb. How do you let yourself ever love like that again, once you eventually manage to pick up the pieces of your shattered heart off the ground?

Love looks different to us now than it did before September 5, 2016. It's much more intentional and deep than before. I've heard it said, "Where there is deep grief, there was great love." We have certainly experienced deep grief, and we indeed had great love for our sweet KB, just as our heavenly Father grieves over his children when they are lost, because his love for us is immeasurable.

In the days and weeks following our loss, as people were sharing images and memories of Katie on social media, the phrase "live and love like KB" became recurrent. There is actually a feature film in the making about her story titled *Kind Katie*. What a beautiful testimony to the way she lived and loved. As we continued processing our great loss, we asked ourselves, *Are we living and loving well?* and *Are we helping others to do that?* In pondering this, we felt God nudge us toward making this our ministry, and in January 2017, only four short months after the darkest days of our lives, Live and

Love Ministries was born. Our mission is to live life to the fullest and to love the Father and others well.

Mark 12:28-34[5]

28 *One of the teachers of the law came and heard them debating. Noticing that Jesus had given them a good answer, he asked him, "Of all the commandments, which is the most important?"*

29 *"The most important one," answered Jesus, "is this: 'Hear, O Israel: The Lord our God, the Lord is one.* **30** *Love the Lord your God with all your heart and with all your soul and with all your mind and with all your strength.'* **31** *The second is this: 'Love your neighbor as yourself.' There is no commandment greater than these."*

32 *"Well said, teacher," the man replied. "You are right in saying that God is one and there is no other but him.* **33** *To love him with all your heart, with all your understanding and with all your strength, and to love your neighbor as yourself is more important than all burnt offerings and sacrifices."*

34 *When Jesus saw that he had answered wisely, he said to him, "You are not far from the kingdom of God." And from then on no one dared ask him any more questions.*

The gospel's command, in simplest terms, is this: Love God, Love Others. This is what we are called to, as children of God. For us, this simply means doing all we can to fill this broken world with as much Christ-like, unconditional love as possible. We will certainly fall short at times, but can you imagine how different this world would be if people quit hurling insults and spewing hate and began simply caring for one another? You don't have to agree with someone to treat them with love and kindness. It is our goal to inspire others to live well and love well, even on the days when it's especially challenging.

REFLECTION QUESTIONS:

- When you have experienced loss, how did fear affect you in the aftermath? How were you able to overcome that fear in order to move forward?
- How has the loss you've experienced in your life affected the way you love others who are hurting?
- Are you loving God and others well? What are some ways you can inspire others to do that?

CHAPTER VII

LAUGH

"Laughter is God's hand on the shoulder
of a troubled world."

- Bettenell Huntznicker

...a time to weep, and a time to laugh;
a time to mourn, and a time to dance;

Ecclesiastes 3:4[1]

If you've just recently experienced deep loss, you're probably thinking, "You've got to be kidding me. Laugh?" We totally get it and your feelings are completely understandable and justifiable, but don't dismiss this chapter. First, it's a pretty short chapter, therefore it won't take you that long to read. Second, it truly is an important part of the healing process and you *will* get there one day, we promise. Lastly, if for no other reason, laughing is good for you physically, mentally, and emotionally, so let's start there. It stimulates your organs, relieves your stress response, and improves your mood.[2]

Grief is a cruel thing. It can have an adverse effect on us in so many ways. When we're sad we typically don't eat right, sleep well, or feel like exercising. Over time, that can take its toll on us physically. When we experience traumatic situations, our mind has the tendency to deceive us and cause a thousand different thoughts to surface, most of which are typically unrealistic, or just bold-faced lies. To top it off, grief's emotional roller coaster exhausts and worsens our emotional state. There are no easy answers to this, but in time laughter will be a healer.

LETTING YOURSELF LAUGH AGAIN {JASON}

In the days and weeks after losing Katie Beth, I vividly remember sitting in my recliner in the living room and saying out loud, "I don't think I'll ever be happy again." Although this would prove to be false, it felt so true and real. In the depth of my soul, I genuinely believed that my happiness had come to an end. I couldn't even picture or imagine myself laughing. What possibly could cause me to ever laugh again after tragically losing my daughter? One of the most precious people that's walked the planet, someone I love more than anyone else in the world, was gone. Laughing seemed like the most ludicrous thought. Obviously, I don't still carry this weight every day, but there are still moments that laughing is nearly impossible or seems foolish.

In time, I was able to find the humor in things, but to conjure up laughter was difficult because an extremely strong emotion accompanied it: guilt. It felt as if when I laughed or had fun or experienced joy that I was being disloyal to Katie Beth. How could laughing or having fun possibly co-exist with deep pain and loss, especially the loss of my daughter? I felt like I had to continually be sad for the loss in order to honor and be loyal to Katie Beth. I know now that these thoughts aren't logical, but in the middle of the pain it made so much sense. Over time, it became apparent that it was okay to enjoy life and laugh. As a matter of fact, I realized it would be one of the keys to being able to take the next step each day and bring an ounce of healing every once in a while.

The funny thing about this whole struggle is that one of the most memorable physical characteristics of Katie Beth is her laugh. She loved life and loved to laugh. She'd want us to continue doing the same. There are nights when Amy and I will lay in the bed and watch a handful of short clips of *The Tonight Show* with Jimmy Fallon, old *Saturday Night Live* skits, or some other funny videos. Sometimes we find ourselves laughing so hard that we're crying. Some nights this is just the right medicine for our weary hearts and we can see light breaking through the fog, making the way a little bit easier to travel.

As a family, we have tried to be intentional about finding ways to laugh again. One of the areas that could have been easy for us to avoid was playing games. As was mentioned in the first chapter, family game night was at the top of Katie Beth's favorite family activities list. It's one of our last family memories with her and the emotions that playing games conjures up can be hard. We have chosen to enter back into that tradition, in order to remember those fun times and laugh together. So many times we want to avoid the things that make us remember, even the good, happy things. What we have come to learn is that when we use those things as an opportunity to laugh and experience joy, God begins to redeem the places where the enemy desires to steal our joy.

TWO SIDES OF THE SAME COIN {AMY}

The day after KB's accident, I received a Facebook message from another stranger that turned out to be a special soul-tie. In this message, Cathy Semeria explained that she had lost her daughter tragically in a car accident just a few months prior (actually on Katie's birthday) and she understood the journey Jason and I were currently on. Cathy's daughter Christina (affectionately known as Tini) had been traveling back to the University of Georgia in Athens with a car full of friends when their accident happened. Four of the five girls in the car died that night, and life changed forever for the girls' families. Even in her brokenness, Cathy was reaching out to minister to me.

> **2 Corinthians 1:4**[3]
> *He comforts us in all our troubles so that we can comfort others. When they are troubled, we will be able to give them the same comfort God has given us.*

I had the honor of meeting Cathy in person when I went to hear her speak at a church event in Atlanta a few months after Katie's accident. She spoke some words that evening that have stuck with me on this grief journey. "Joy and sorrow are two sides of the same coin. You can't really experience true, deep joy if you haven't experienced deep sorrow." Most of us just want the deep joy part, but we run from the idea of deep sorrow. I did, at least. Yet, here I was, in the middle of truly deep sorrow, wondering if I would ever experience any joy again. Cathy's daughter Tini wrote this on her blog before her accident, "Joy is a difficult thing. It is not, however, to be mistaken with happiness. Happiness is based on circumstances. Joy is an orientation of the heart. It remains even in the most strenuous moments, and has no barriers or limitations. It is from a God of unconditional and everlasting love."[4] Words of wisdom from a beautiful soul.

Nine months after losing Katie, our son married his long time sweetheart, and we truly understood the double-sided coin Cathy had spoken about. We had such joy in our hearts for Jacob and Rachel as they were entering into this new season of life, yet we couldn't ignore the pain of knowing that Katie should have been there celebrating with us. As a part of their wedding, Jacob and Rachel chose to honor Katie Beth and their close friend Jordan who had recently lost her fight with cancer. At one point in the ceremony, they both walked to a table that had pictures of Katie Beth and Jordan and took a minute to pray. This was an extremely emotional moment where tears were shed by many. Though important and appropriate, they couldn't *stay* there; they had to keep moving, as that day was ultimately a joyous occasion to celebrate their love for one another. Every special occasion or family event since has this same double-edged feeling. Joy. And sorrow.

Our family loves to laugh and have fun. Ask anyone who knows the Carters. Katie Beth had this amazing, deep-from-your-soul kind of laugh and she laughed a lot. After losing her laugh, we wondered if any of us would ever laugh or have fun again. Meister Eckhart says, "In the heart of the Trinity the Father laughs and gives birth to the Son. The Son laughs back at the Father and gives birth to the Spirit. The whole Trinity laughs and gives birth to us." Slowly, but surely, God brought joy (and laughter) back into our hearts and home. Honestly, it feels strange at first, laughing, after so much sorrow and crying. Be patient. Joy will come. Laughter will come. And it's okay. There are two sides to the coin.

REFLECTION QUESTIONS:

- Have you experienced a time in your life where you thought you might never be happy again? Did you find it difficult to give yourself permission to be happy again? Why is it important to do this?
- How do you define happiness versus joy? How can we rediscover joy in the midst of dark days?
- How do joy and sorrow relate to one another? Are there times where you have experienced both sides of the same coin? What did God teach you in those moments?

CHAPTER VIII

LEGACY

"Carve your name on hearts, not tombstones.
A legacy is etched into the minds of others
and the stories they share about you."
- Shannon L. Alder

We've heard true stories from our fathers
about our rich heritage.
We will continue to tell our children
and not hide from the rising generation
the great marvels of our God—
his miracles and power that have brought us all this far.
Psalm 78:3-4[1]

SECUNDARIA CONMEMORATIVA
KATIE BETH CARTER

Outside of a large red building, painted by the hands of invested hearts, stands a sign that tells a story much deeper than the few letters that fill its space. It's a story much larger than the life it commemorates; larger than the community who came together to build the school's walls; larger than the citizens of Tomás Borge, Nicaragua that the school serves. This story is about a God who is about life, love, and redemption. This story reflects His ability to transform the unthinkable into something glorious. This story is about trading beauty for ashes.

Coach EK Slaughter's Leadership class, Heritage High School's student-led organization now known as Impact2One, had a dream that came to fruition. After over a year of planning, raising support, and multiple visits to Nicaragua, the Katie Beth Carter Memorial Institute stands in the heart of Tomás Borge. Each week, children are learning English. Eight mothers gather in an open-air room and learn to sew, not only for their families, but in hopes to develop a profitable skill. Students are learning how to become leaders in their community, and children with special needs are no longer treated as marginalized citizens, but as children who are welcomed and loved.

This community that once served as the dump of the nearby city of Leon is now a place of cultivation, learning, and promise. Citizens of Tomás Borge, who previously spent lifetimes filtering through the greater country's garbage as a means to get by, are now welcoming rejuvenation and hope into their world.

In August 2016, just a year prior to breaking ground, Heritage High School Principal Ronnie Bradford approached Coach EK Slaughter about partnering with, and supporting, a foreign school. Slaughter brought this to his Leadership class, who then began researching for schools to partner with. Through a series of connections, the class came in contact with an organization which had recently bought a 9-acre plot in Tomás Borge, Nicaragua with the hopes of building a school to serve this impoverished community.

The Leadership class soon began to question what it would cost to build a school instead of partnering with one that already existed. The class came in contact with Jeremy Barcenas, a leader of an organization established in Tomás Borge with a goal to "bring love, faith and hope to the neediest by raising morale, instilling values, teaching skills, developing leaders and preaching with our actions to deliver a renewed and visionary generation to the future."[2] The Leadership class from Heritage High School, created their own service organization (Impact2One) with a mission committed to a lifetime partnership with the people of Tomás Borge through loving, providing, and inspiring each other to change the world one person at a time.[3] And just as the class contemplated the possibility of a commitment to Nicaragua, on September 5, 2016, Katie Beth Carter had her accident.

Over the course of the following three months, a determined team of Heritage High School students presented to local businesses, orchestrated fundraisers, and raised over $60,000 in support. Because of Katie Beth's well renowned intentionality, her desperate desire to serve, and her love for teaching and inspiring children, the class, along with Barcenas, didn't think twice about erecting the school as a way to honor Katie Beth's legacy of love.

REBUILDING THE RUINS

Isaiah 61:4[4]

And they will rebuild the ancient ruins
and restore the places long devastated;
And they will renew the ruined cities that have been
devastated for generations.

There it is, a real life example of the promises of God being fulfilled. A community that is one of the poorest places we have ever seen, that sits on top of what used to be the dump where the city's trash was burned, now has hope for the future. This place was the *ashes* that Isaiah references; and now, in the middle of the community, a piece of property named Open Heavens sits with a brand new school named after our daughter. These people have expressed to us their pain of feeling forgotten by the world. Because of this, we are committed to fostering our relationship with the people of Tomás Borge. This is a place where life-change is beginning to happen. Children are being educated, mothers are learning to sew in order to make money for their families, a water tank provides clean water to the locals, and special needs students who had previously been hidden away are now being taught life skills and given a basic education. In addition, long and short-term housing units are being built for those who feel called to serve the community of Tomás Borge. These ruins are being rebuilt and renewed, but most of all, this is instilling hope into the hearts of people who have lived amidst hopelessness for far too long.

You see, no matter the pain you feel, God can use it. Not only will He use it, but He promises to make it beautiful. At the risk of being misheard, we want to be clear: this doesn't mean that you'll never feel the pain or that the heartache will go away. Trust me, there are still plenty of days we find it hard to function because we miss our girl. There will always be a hole and we will always carry some semblance of brokenness. The construction of a school in Nicaragua named after Katie Beth alone will never take that away. But, it helps us to see that there is purpose in our pain. The day we lost Katie Beth, our prayer was that our pain wouldn't be wasted. To that, our God has been faithful in every sense.

LIVING OUT LEGACY

Legacy is about who you choose to be *today*, especially when things get tough. Today it may be as simple as making the decision to not quit. For us, this was the first step, and honestly all we were capable of in those first few months. We made a decision early on that we were going to live even if that meant simply putting one foot in front of the other, facing the day one moment at a time. These choices are the roots that you drive into the ground that will one day transform you into an Oak and create legacy.

Your legacy is established in the small, every day, consistent actions you choose to take. Legacy can look like a school in another country or legacy can look like how you communicate to one person in your home with love and compassion. It's about panning for the gold in the muck and mire of the raging torrent of pain you live in. At first glance, it just looks like a bunch of rock and mud and water. However, if you will step into the current and begin the long, arduous process of sifting out all of the less valuable junk, you will see it. The light will hit it and it will glimmer. It's the gold beneath all the dirt... the light breaking through the fog. Regardless of your loss and pain or the circumstances surrounding it, you have to go find the gold beneath it all, those things that hold great value and will change a life. That is what will bring purpose to your pain and leave a legacy that will last long after you're gone.

The fact that Katie Beth's life has impacted, and continues to impact, so many people still astounds us. Katie never accomplished "great things" from an earthly perspective. She simply lived her life in a way that caused people to take notice. Katie Beth invested in people better than most anyone I've ever known—and boy, did she love Jesus with all she was. Because of this, her life here on earth made an impact on others in ways she would have never imagined. Katie Beth decided to live her life in a way that put God and people first. In the end she has, and will continue to leave, a legacy she never thought she could. That legacy, the one she'd probably deem impossible, is changing lives all over the world. Now, our family has a choice in how we'll use our pain and how we'll share our story.

James 3:13[5]

Do you want to be counted wise, to build a reputation for wisdom? Here's what you do: Live well, live wisely, live humbly. It's the way you live, not the way you talk, that counts.

How we handle victory, how we navigate defeat, how we respond to tragedy and hardship—it all matters! It matters to you and it affects so many people, even those you'll never know. Remember, the loss you have endured, and the pain you feel, has a deeper purpose. It's not just about the pain. If you'll allow God to use you through it, He will make you into an Oak of Righteousness. Don't let the loss define you, but let it be the very thing that propels you into becoming who He wants you to be and what will begin to shape your legacy.

Yes, losing Katie Beth will always be a part of who we are, but we have to make a choice as to whether we will allow the pain and heartache to dominate our story or if we will allow God to rebuild these ruins for His glory. Being made into an Oak is a lifelong process. We will always be on this journey, but our intentional choices to show others compassion, to live and love well even on the days it's hard, to bring hope to those who are desperately searching for something to believe in, and to point people back to Jesus are what will shape our legacy. These things are the reason for Katie Beth's legacy and this standard is no different for the rest of us. Those intentional choices are like the acorns of an oak tree, the fruit we produce that will ultimately grow into another Oak that will produce more fruit. In the words of William James, "The great use of life is to spend it for something that will outlast it."

People all around us are wounded and hurting and have experienced a myriad of losses. The Father's heart is to bring restoration and healing to a very broken world and His plan has always been to use imperfect and broken people to accomplish this mission. It's the promise found in **Isaiah 61:4**: *"And they will rebuild the ancient ruins and restore the places long devastated; And they will renew the ruined cities that have been devastated for generations."*

"Rebuilding Ruins" can sound like an impossible and overwhelming feat, but it's actually quite simple. Jesus provides the ultimate example, but His disciples, twelve ordinary men, did the same thing and changed the world. It doesn't require lots of money, multiple degrees, major influence, or even deep levels of spirituality. It's about being aware of the people around you who are hurting and broken, and giving them a hope for the future by simply loving them with your actions. It looks like:

> Befriending the person who needs a friend
>
> Mowing the yard for the lady who just lost her husband
>
> Choosing to change generational family patterns
>
> Investing in the child who lost a mom or dad by spending

time with them

Traveling to an impoverished neighborhood or country and serving them

Granting forgiveness in a broken relationship

Lending a shoulder to cry on or an ear to listen

Loving people right where they are

Rebuilding the ruins really is about finding the gold that is hidden in your loss—and finding the gold in others—and then bringing it into the light. How you choose to do it is up to you, but this isn't the most important part of the rebuilding process. The most important part is that you actually do it—that you begin, one step at a time, one choice at a time, one person at a time, allowing God to redeem your loss.

What part will you play? What will you do with the loss you've endured? What will you do with the time you've been given? What will you leave inside of people? Your decision *could* be the difference in how people you know, and those you may never know, live their lives.

God created us each uniquely. Our journeys will be unique. Our losses are unique as well. Whatever your journey or loss may be, God *can* and *will* redeem it, *if* you let Him. The possibilities are endless; don't let your pain be wasted. He is growing us into those Mighty Oaks. He is using us to rebuild ruins. There are plenty of ruins to be rebuilt. And when our time here on earth is done, may it be said of us that we lived fully and loved well, just like Jesus. So, let our prayer be: Oaks and ruins, Lord. Oaks and Ruins.

REFLECTION QUESTIONS:

- What does the word legacy bring to your mind?
- What kind of legacy do you hope to create with your life? How can your pain and loss be used to help form that legacy?
- Have you asked God to form you into an Oak of Righteousness and use you to rebuild ruins? Will you allow him to redeem your loss for a greater glory?

INTRODUCTION

1. Isaiah 61:3-4, a combination of New International Version and New King James Version

   NKJV (New King James Version): Scripture taken from the New King James Version®. Copyright © 1982 by Thomas Nelson. Used by permission. All rights reserved.

   THE HOLY BIBLE, NEW INTERNATIONAL VERSION®, NIV® Copyright © 2011 by Biblica, Inc.® Used by permission. All rights reserved worldwide.

LOSS

1. Psalm 34:18, New International Version

   THE HOLY BIBLE, NEW INTERNATIONAL VERSION®, NIV® Copyright © 2011 by Biblica, Inc.® Used by permission. All rights reserved worldwide.

LISTEN

1. Proverbs 20:12, Christian Standard Bible

   The Christian Standard Bible (CSB) Copyright © 2017 by Holman Bible Publishers. Used by permission. Christian Standard Bible®, and CSB® are federally registered trademarks of Holman Bible Publishers, all rights reserved.

2. "Consecrating Empathy – Part 1 and Part 2." *Conversations with John Eldredge and the Team at Ransomed Heart* from Ransomed Heart, March 2018, http://www.ransomedheart.com/podcast/consecrating-empathy-part-1 and http://www.ransomedheart.com/podcast/consecrating-empathy-part-2.

3. Greg Laurie, "An Evening of Hope: A Conversation about Pain with Steven Curtis Chapman (Nov. 19, 2009)." *Greg's Blog*, Harvest Christian Fellowship, https://greg.harvest.org/a-conversation-about-pain-and-grief-with-steven-curtis-chapman.

4. Psalm 42:9-11, Christian Standard Bible

5. Havilah Cunnington, "Day 4: Get off the Couch (2014)," *I Do Hard Things*. Havilah's Blog, Wordpress. http://havilahcunnington.com/day-4.

6. Schwiebert, Pat, and Chuck DeKlyen. *Tear Soup: A Recipe for Healing After Loss*. Grief Watch, 2009.

LOOK

1. Ephesians 1:18, New International Version

2. Rushnell, Squire. *When God Winks: How the Power of Coincidence Guides Your Life*. Simon & Schuster Australia, 2002.

LEARN

1. Psalm 32:8, New International Version

2. Luke 22:39-43, Christian Standard Bible

3. Platt, David. *Radical: Taking Back Your Faith from the American Dream*. Multnomah Books, 2010, pp. 34-36.

4. Genesis 1:26-27, Holman Christian Standard Bible

HCSB are taken from the Holman Christian Standard Bible®, Copyright © 1999, 2000, 2002, 2003, 2009 by Holman Bible Publishers. Used by permission. Holman Christian Standard Bible®, Holman CSB®, and HCSB® are federally registered trademarks of Holman Bible Publishers.

5. Luke 8:40-48, Holman Christian Standard Bible

Holman Christian Standard Bible, Scripture quotations marked HCSB are taken from the Holman Christian Standard Bible®, Copyright © 1999, 2000, 2002, 2003, 2009 by Holman Bible Publishers. Used by permission. Holman Christian Standard Bible®, Holman CSB®, and HCSB® are federally registered trademarks of Holman Bible Publishers.

LIVE

1. John 10:10, Holman Christian Standard Bible

Holman Christian Standard Bible, Scripture quotations marked HCSB are taken from the Holman Christian Standard Bible®, Copyright © 1999, 2000, 2002, 2003, 2009 by Holman Bible Publishers. Used by permission. Holman Christian Standard Bible®, Holman CSB®, and HCSB® are federally registered trademarks of Holman Bible Publishers.

2. Ephesians 6:12, Holman Christian Standard Bible

Holman Christian Standard Bible, Scripture quotations marked HCSB are taken from the Holman Christian Standard Bible®, Copyright © 1999, 2000, 2002, 2003, 2009 by Holman Bible Publishers. Used by permission. Holman Christian Standard Bible®, Holman CSB®, and HCSB® are federally registered trademarks of Holman Bible Publishers.

3. Eldredge, John. *Epic: The Story God is Telling and the Role That is Yours to Play.* Thomas Nelson Incorporated, 2007, p. 15.

4. Philippians 3:7-11, Christian Standard Bible

The Christian Standard Bible (CSB) Copyright © 2017 by Holman Bible Publishers. Used by permission. Christian Standard Bible®, and CSB® are federally registered trademarks of Holman Bible Publishers, all rights reserved.

5. Tolkien, J.R.R. *The Fellowship of the Ring*. Allen & Unwin, 1954.

6. Psalm 103:7, New International Version

THE HOLY BIBLE, NEW INTERNATIONAL VERSION®, NIV® Copyright © 2011 by Biblica, Inc.® Used by permission. All rights reserved worldwide.

7. Genesis 50:19-20, New International Version

THE HOLY BIBLE, NEW INTERNATIONAL VERSION®, NIV® Copyright © 1973, 1978, 1984, 2011 by Biblica, Inc.® Used by permission. All rights reserved worldwide.

LOVE

1. 1 Corinthians 16:14, New International Version

THE HOLY BIBLE, NEW INTERNATIONAL VERSION®, NIV® Copyright © 2011 by Biblica, Inc.® Used by permission. All rights reserved worldwide.

2. "Consecrating Empathy – Part 1 and Part 2." *Conversations with John Eldredge and the Team at Ransomed Heart* from Ransomed Heart, March 2018, http://www.ransomedheart.com/podcast/consecrating-empathy-part-1 and http://www.ransomedheart.com/podcast/consecrating-empathy-part-2.

3. Romans 12:1-2, Holman Christian Standard Bible

Holman Christian Standard Bible, Scripture quotations marked HCSB are taken from the Holman Christian Standard Bible®, Copyright © 1999, 2000, 2002, 2003, 2009 by Holman Bible Publishers. Used by permission. Holman Christian Standard Bible®, Holman CSB®, and HCSB® are federally registered trademarks of Holman Bible Publishers.

4. I John 4:8, King James Version

Public Domain

5. Mark 12:28-34, New International Version

THE HOLY BIBLE, NEW INTERNATIONAL VERSION®, NIV®

LAUGH

1. Ecclesiastes 3:4, King James Version

   NKJV (New King James Version): Scripture taken from the New King James Version®. Copyright © 1982 by Thomas Nelson. Used by permission. All rights reserved.

2. The Mayo Clinic Staff. "Stress Relief from Laughter? It's No Joke." 2016. https://www.mayoclinic.org/healthy-lifestyle/stress-management/in-depth/stress-relief/art-20044456.

3. 2 Corinthians 1:4, New Living Translation

   New Living Translation (NLV) Scripture quotations marked NLT are taken from the Holy Bible, New Living Translation, copyright © 1996, 2004, 2015 by Tyndale House Foundation. Used by permission of Tyndale House Publishers, Inc., Carol Stream, Illinois 60188. All rights reserved.

4. Christina Semeria, "A Spark in the Dark (2016)," *A Stirring Heart*. Wordpress. https://christinasemeria.wordpress.com/?s=a+spark+in+the+dark.

LEGACY

1. Psalm 78:4, The Passion Translation

   Scripture quotations marked TPT are from The Passion Translation®. Copyright © 2017, 2018 by Passion & Fire Ministries, Inc. Used by permission. All rights reserved. ThePassionTranslation.com.

2. http://nicamericanmissions.org

3. https://www.impact2one.org

4. Isaiah 61:4, New International Version

   THE HOLY BIBLE, NEW INTERNATIONAL VERSION®, NIV® Copyright © 2011 by Biblica, Inc.® Used by permission. All rights reserved worldwide.

5. James 3:13, The Message

    Scripture taken from The Message. Copyright © 1993, 1994, 1995, 1996, 2000, 2001, 2002. Used by permission of NavPress Publishing Group.

BOOKS

Child Loss: The Heartbreak and the Hope by Clara Hinton

Through The Eyes Of A Lion by Levi Lusko

Tear Soup: A Recipe for Healing After Loss by Chuck DeKlyen and Pat Schwiebert

A Grace Disguised: How the Soul Grows Through Loss by Gerald Lawson Sittser

A Grace Revealed: How God Redeems the Story of Your Life by Gerald Lawson Sittser

Choosing To SEE: A Journey of Struggle and Hope by Mary Beth Chapman

The Broken Way by Ann Voskamp

When God Winks at You: How God Speaks Directly to You Through the Power of Coincidence by SQuire D. Rushnell

Epic: The Story God Is Telling And The Role That is Yours To Play by John Eldredge

WEBSITES

www.liveandloveministries.com

www.kindkatie.com

www.impact2one.org

www.pastorrick.com

www.compassionatefriends.org

www.christinasemeria.org

LIVE & LOVE
M I N I S T R I E S

Live and Love Ministries exists to encourage and inspire others to live life to the fullest (John 10:10) and love the Father and others well (Matthew 22:37-39). Through our story and experiences we desire to empower individuals in establishing and growing deeper and more meaningful relationships with God and others.

Follow us:
Instagram: @liveandloveministries
Facebook: facebook.com/liveandloveministries
Email: info@liveandloveministries.com
Website: www.liveandloveministries.com

If you are interested in booking Jason and Amy to speak at your church, organization, or event, visit the "Speaking" page on the Live and Love Ministries website.

CPSIA information can be obtained
at www.ICGtesting.com
Printed in the USA
LVHW01s1145231018
594463LV00003B/3/P